Business Guides on the Go

"Business Guides on the Go" presents cutting-edge insights from practice on particular topics within the fields of business, management, and finance. Written by practitioners and experts in a concise and accessible form the series provides professionals with a general understanding and a first practical approach to latest developments in business strategy, leadership, operations, HR management, innovation and technology management, marketing or digitalization. Students of business administration or management will also benefit from these practical guides for their future occupation/careers.

These Guides suit the needs of today's fast reader.

Adrian Vogler

Digital Management Practice

Mastering Exponential Change with Collective and Artificial Intelligence

Adrian Vogler
Winkelhaid, Germany

ISSN 2731-4758 ISSN 2731-4766 (electronic)
Business Guides on the Go
ISBN 978-3-662-68352-1 ISBN 978-3-662-68353-8 (eBook)
https://doi.org/10.1007/978-3-662-68353-8

© The Editor(s) (if applicable) and The Author(s), under exclusive license to Springer-Verlag GmbH, DE, part of Springer Nature 2024

This work is subject to copyright. All rights are solely and exclusively licensed by the Publisher, whether the whole or part of the material is concerned, specifically the rights of translation, reprinting, reuse of illustrations, recitation, broadcasting, reproduction on microfilms or in any other physical way, and transmission or information storage and retrieval, electronic adaptation, computer software, or by similar or dissimilar methodology now known or hereafter developed.

The use of general descriptive names, registered names, trademarks, service marks, etc. in this publication does not imply, even in the absence of a specific statement, that such names are exempt from the relevant protective laws and regulations and therefore free for general use.

The publisher, the authors, and the editors are safe to assume that the advice and information in this book are believed to be true and accurate at the date of publication. Neither the publisher nor the authors or the editors give a warranty, expressed or implied, with respect to the material contained herein or for any errors or omissions that may have been made. The publisher remains neutral with regard to jurisdictional claims in published maps and institutional affiliations.

This Springer imprint is published by the registered company Springer-Verlag GmbH, DE, part of Springer Nature.
The registered company address is: Heidelberger Platz 3, 14197 Berlin, Germany

Paper in this product is recyclable

Preface

Dear Readers,

I am very pleased to present my book "Digital Management Practice". At a time when digitalisation and exponential change are fundamentally transforming the working environment of companies and managers, it is more important than ever to apply Peter F. Drucker's proven management principles to the new challenges.

In this book, I have addressed the question of how managers and knowledge workers can work more effectively with the help of collective and artificial intelligence to counteract the effects of exponential change. I am concerned not only with the use of concrete technologies, but also with the question of how the manager can optimally use the knowledge and skills of knowledge workers.

I pay special attention to the combination of proven management principles and new technologies. It is important to me not only to point out short-term solutions, but also to consider medium- and long-term issues. Because only in this way can companies and managers continue to be successful in the future.

I cordially invite you to embark on an exciting journey through digital management practice and look forward to mastering the challenges of the future together with you.

Yours sincerely,

Winkelhaid, Germany   Adrian Vogler

Contents

1 Introduction 1

Part I Digitalisation and Exponential Change

2 The Digitalisation 5
   2.1 Digitisation 5
      2.1.1 Digitisation 1.0 6
      2.1.2 Digitisation 2.0 6
      2.1.3 Digitisation 3.0 7
      2.1.4 Digitisation 4.0 7
      2.1.5 Industry 4.0 7
   2.2 Acceleration 8
   2.3 Exponential Change 9
   2.4 Effects and Requirements 10
   References 11

3 The Knowledge Worker 13
   3.1 Knowledge Work and Knowledge Workers 13
   3.2 Tool 14
      3.2.1 The Mental System 14
      3.2.2 The Limitations of the Mental System 15

3.3		Change	18
3.4		Digitisation	19
3.5		Requirements	21
References			23

4 The Manager ... 25
4.1 Role of the Manager ... 25
4.1.1 Tasks ... 25
4.1.2 Tools ... 27
4.1.3 Principles ... 28
4.1.4 Knowledge Workers ... 29
4.2 Change ... 30
4.3 Digitisation ... 31
4.4 Requirements ... 33
Reference ... 34

5 The Company ... 35
5.1 Purpose ... 35
5.2 Change ... 36
5.3 Digitisation ... 37
5.3.1 Innovation Management ... 38
5.3.2 Business Model ... 39
5.4 Exponential Change ... 39
5.5 Requirements ... 41
References ... 42

Part II Collective Intelligence as a System 3

6 Presentation of System 3: The Concept of Collective Intelligence ... 45
6.1 Definition ... 45
6.2 Delimitation ... 47
6.3 Fields of Application ... 48
Reference ... 51

7 Benefits of System 3: The Collective Intelligence ... 53
7.1 Benefits for the Knowledge Worker ... 53
7.1.1 Distortions in Perception ... 53
7.1.2 Overconfidence ... 54
7.1.3 Availability Heuristic ... 55
7.1.4 Influence of Emotions on Thinking ... 56
7.1.5 Confirmation Error ... 57
7.1.6 Framing Effect ... 57
7.1.7 Anchor Heuristics ... 58
7.2 Benefits for the Manager ... 59
7.2.1 Management of the New ... 59
7.2.2 Management of the Existing ... 61
7.2.3 Organisation of the Work ... 62
7.2.4 Benefits in the Context of the Principles ... 63
7.3 Benefits for the Company ... 64
References ... 65

8 Concrete Application of System 3: The Collective Intelligence ... 67
8.1 Requirements and Prerequisites ... 67
8.1.1 Technological Requirements ... 67
8.1.2 Organisational Requirements ... 69
8.1.3 Employee Competencies ... 70
8.2 Implementation ... 71
8.2.1 Planning and Conception ... 72
8.2.2 Implement the First Project ... 74
8.2.3 Integration into Existing Processes ... 76
8.3 Evaluation and Optimisation ... 77
8.3.1 Evaluate Results ... 77
8.3.2 Use of the Knowledge Gained ... 78
8.3.3 Continuous Improvement ... 78
8.4 Further Application Examples ... 79
References ... 81

Part III Artificial Intelligence as a System 4

9 Presentation of System 4: The Concept of Artificial Intelligence 87
- 9.1 Definition 87
- 9.2 Delimitation 90
- 9.3 Fields of Application 91
- Reference 93

10 Benefits of System 4: Artificial Intelligence 95
- 10.1 Benefits for the Knowledge Worker 95
  - 10.1.1 Distortions in Perception 95
  - 10.1.2 Overconfidence 97
  - 10.1.3 Availability Heuristic 98
  - 10.1.4 Influence of Emotions on Thinking 99
  - 10.1.5 Confirmation Error 100
  - 10.1.6 Framing Effect 101
  - 10.1.7 Anchor Heuristics 102
- 10.2 Benefits for the Manager 102
  - 10.2.1 Management of the New 102
  - 10.2.2 Management of the Existing 103
  - 10.2.3 Organisation of the Work 104
  - 10.2.4 Benefits in the Context of the Principles 106
- 10.3 Benefits for the Company 107
- References 107

11 Concrete Application of System 4: Artificial Intelligence 109
- 11.1 Requirements and Prerequisites 109
  - 11.1.1 Technological Requirements 109
  - 11.1.2 Organisational Requirements 110
  - 11.1.3 Data Protection and Ethical Considerations 112
- 11.2 Employee Competences 118
  - 11.2.1 Technical Skills and Expertise 119
  - 11.2.2 Collaboration and Communication 120

	11.2.3	Critical Thinking and Problem-Solving 122

        11.2.3 Critical Thinking and Problem-Solving 122
        11.2.4 Willingness to Change and Ability to Learn 123
  11.3 Implementation 124
        11.3.1 Planning and Conception 125
        11.3.2 Implement the First Project 127
        11.3.3 Integration into Existing Processes 128
  11.4 Evaluation and Optimisation 129
        11.4.1 Evaluate Results 129
        11.4.2 Use of the Knowledge Gained 130
        11.4.3 Continuous Improvement 130
  11.5 Further Application Examples 131
  References 133

12 Conclusion and Recommendations for Action 135
  12.1 Review and Consolidation 135
  12.2 The Relevance of System 3 and System 4 136
  12.3 People and Technology in Management 136
  12.4 Recommendations for Action and Next Steps 136
  12.5 Final Thoughts 136

13 Practical Examples of AI Tools and Further Literature 137
  13.1 Appendix 1: Working with ChatGPT 138
        13.1.1 Practical Example 139
        13.1.2 Technical Terms 146
        13.1.3 Division of Labour 147
  13.2 Appendix 2: Working with IBM Watson 149
        13.2.1 Cognitive Computing and Watson 150
        13.2.2 Cognitive Computing and Big Data Analytics . 151
        13.2.3 Platform and Software 154
        13.2.4 Concept of the System 155
        13.2.5 The Process of Implementation 162
  13.3 Appendix 3: Further Reading 170
  References 203

About the Author

Adrian Vogler With over 30 years of experience in the IT industry and as a manager, Adrian Vogler has gained extensive knowledge and experience in the field of management. He has worked in and organised small teams, as well as large-scale IT projects with several hundred project staff.

As a leader, staff development has been a particular concern of his and he has always followed the strengths-based approach. As a member of the Peter Drucker Society Europe, he has exchanged ideas with representatives from other organisations and has himself used the tools of collective and artificial intelligence he described in his projects.

He has more than 25 years of experience in writing technical books and has already written on various management and IT topics.

Adrian Vogler holds a degree in administration and a Master of Science in practical computer science with a focus on AI and Industry 4.0. Since 2016, he has successfully participated in tenders for research and funding projects, e.g. from the BMBF, with project consortia that he organised.

1

Introduction

Few changes have such a lasting impact on civilisation as a change in the principle on which the organisation of work is based. [Druc02]

This quote by Peter F. Drucker, one of the most famous management pioneers of the twentieth century, is deliberately placed at the beginning of this book. For indeed, today we are at a turning point where digitalisation and exponential change are changing the way we work and do business. Companies need to adapt to the fact that traditional management methods may no longer be sufficient to succeed in today's dynamic environment.

This book is about responding to how the manager can make himself and the knowledge workers in his organisation effective in managing change and seizing opportunities. Technology plays an important role in this, but only to fulfil the manager's task of delivering business value while nurturing and developing people (see Fig. 1.1).

The combination of Peter F. Drucker's question with Daniel Kahneman's insights into the strengths and weaknesses of our mental system forms the basis for this book. Daniel Kahneman's concept distinguishes between two systems of thought: System 1 and System 2.

System 1 is the fast and intuitive thinking system that allows us to react quickly to situations and make decisions without consciously thinking about it. It is based on experiences and expectations stored in our brain. System 2 is the slow and reflective thinking system that allows us to think consciously and solve complex problems. It requires conscious attention and concentration to use it.

The book builds on these findings and develops a concept that highlights the benefits of collective and artificial intelligence. This concept is described with the terms System 3 and System 4 and expands the thought processes of the knowledge worker. It enables completely new results in dealing with the abundance of structured and unstructured data in a Big Data system.

The book is divided into three parts. In Part 1, I discuss digitalisation and exponential change and explain the impact on companies, managers and knowledge workers. Part 2 deals with the topic of collective intelligence and how the System 3 tool can be used to increase the effectiveness of knowledge workers. In Part 3, I present the System 4 tool, which is based on artificial intelligence and helps to tap the potential of Big Data.

I hope that my book will help you as a manager and leader to understand the new rules of the game in the digital world and to clarify the strengths and weaknesses of both human and digital players. On this basis, you can structure your organisation to meet the demands of your customers, develop your employees and manage the impact of the company on the environment.

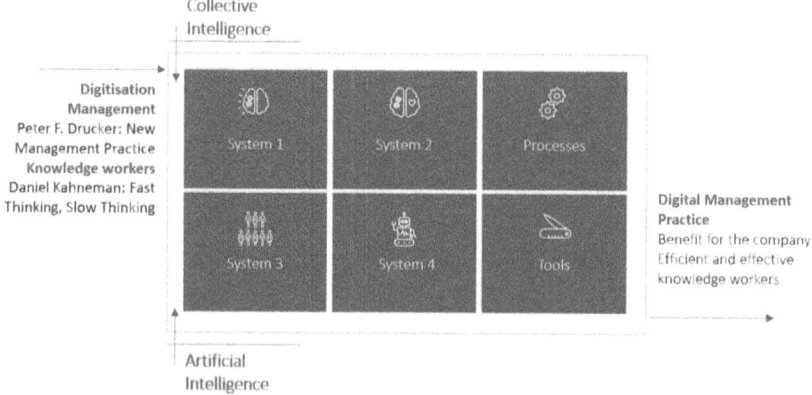

Fig. 1.1 The system structure for the book

Part I

Digitalisation and Exponential Change

Digitisation is not just a shift from analogue to digital tools and methods, but rather a revolution in the way we think and act, in the way we organise and run our business.—Fredmund Malik [Mana19]

1.1 Outlook on Part I

Part I of the book begins with Chap. 2 with digitalisation as an overarching theme and considers it as a fundamental development that influences all other areas.

Building on this, Chap. 3 looks at the knowledge worker as an important component of the modern knowledge society, who is also faced with new demands as a result of digitalisation and the accompanying change in the world of work.

Subsequently, Chap. 4 focuses on the manager, who plays an important role as a driving force in the company organisation and who also faces new challenges as a result of digitalisation.

Finally, the last chapter (Chap. 5) of Part I looks at the company as an entity that is affected by digitalisation and needs to adapt accordingly.

2

The Digitalisation

2.1 Digitisation

Digitalisation is the biggest revolution since the invention of printing. It is fundamentally and sustainably changing the way we live, work, communicate and do business. The impact on society is enormous and we will have to deal intensively with the challenges and opportunities of this development in the coming years and decades. (Malik, 2019)

Imagine you go to a library and want to find a book. A few decades ago, you had to search the catalogue on paper and then go to a specific shelf to find the book. Today, you go to a computer, type in the title or author and immediately see where the book is. That is an example of what digitisation means: the transformation of analogue information into digital formats.

However, digitalisation is much more than just the transformation of information. It is about applying digital technologies to improve or even redesign business processes, products and services. Digitalisation has changed the way we work, communicate, shop and even how we live our lives. With the fourth industrial revolution, also known as

Digitalisation 4.0, these changes will penetrate even deeper into all areas of our lives.

In the chapter on digitalisation and Digitalisation 4.0, we will look at the impact of these developments on companies and managers. We will look at how companies can optimise their business processes through digital technologies, how the role of the manager is changing and how digital transformation is changing the way companies interact with each other.

2.1.1 Digitisation 1.0

Digitisation 1.0 began in 1946 with the invention of the first mainframe computer called ENIAC (Electronic Numerical Integrator and Computer). With a size of 30 tons and a performance of 5000 computing operations per second, the ENIAC was a breakthrough in computer development. It was originally developed for military purposes to perform ballistic calculations. But it was soon realised that the use of computers could also offer enormous advantages in other areas such as business and science. The introduction of the mainframe was an important step in digitalisation and laid the foundation for the further development of computer technology.

2.1.2 Digitisation 2.0

In the late 1970s, the world experienced a new era of digitalisation when the first personal computer (PC) came onto the market. The Apple II and the Commodore PET made the PC accessible to the mass market for the first time. The introduction of the PC fundamentally changed the way people work, communicate and spend their leisure time. The ability to create, store and edit documents and the ability to search and share information quickly made the PC an indispensable tool for knowledge work. Companies began to realise the advantages of the PC and started to integrate it into their work processes. Digitalisation 2.0 was the beginning of an era in which computers became commonplace not only for scientists and governments but also for companies and private individuals.

2.1.3 Digitisation 3.0

Digitisation 3.0 began with the invention of the first website in 1991 by the British physicist Tim Berners-Lee. This innovation revolutionised the way we share and access information. The ability to publish and share information online made communication between people and businesses around the world easier and faster. The emergence of the World Wide Web also brought a new era of e-commerce, as it was now possible to offer and sell products and services online. Digitisation 3.0 laid the foundation for many of today's technologies, including social media, mobile apps and the increasing interconnectivity of devices and systems.

2.1.4 Digitisation 4.0

The fourth phase of digitalisation, also known as "Industry 4.0", began in 2007 with the introduction of the first iPhone. This phase is characterised by the networking of production processes, machines and systems, which enables increasing automation and optimisation of processes. The combination of artificial intelligence, Big Data and the Internet of Things (IoT) is leading to unprecedented efficiency and speed in manufacturing and the exchange of information. Digitalisation 4.0 has the potential to fundamentally change the way companies and organisations work and bring about new business models.

2.1.5 Industry 4.0

Digitalisation and Industry 4.0 are closely linked. While digitalisation is the prerequisite for Industry 4.0, Industry 4.0 is a consequence of digitalisation. The progressive digitalisation of production processes enables the networking and integration of manufacturing systems as well as the use of Big Data and artificial intelligence to optimise processes and products. Industry 4.0 is thus a development that uses the potential of digitalisation to make industrial production more efficient and flexible. In this context, the aim is to digitalise, network and automate production processes in order to achieve a high degree of flexibility and individualisation in production. This is intended to increase the competitiveness of companies.

2.2 Acceleration

> In the past, it was decades, maybe even generations. Today it is years, sometimes only months. The acceleration of all changes makes every sigmoid curve shrink. (Handy, 1995)

The individual phases of digitalisation have brought about a considerable acceleration of value-creating processes. With the introduction of the first mainframe in 1946 as part of Digitalisation 1.0, it was primarily data storage and processing processes that were automated. This enabled faster processing of data and thus an acceleration of processes.

In Digitalisation 2.0 from 1977, the introduction of the first PC brought computers into people's offices and workplaces for the first time. This made new forms of work possible and automated processes, which also resulted in an acceleration.

With the introduction of the first website in 1991 in Digitalisation 3.0, the internet came into being and with it a global networking of people and machines. This networking opened up new possibilities for cooperation and communication and accelerated the flow of information.

In Digitalisation 4.0 from 2007 onwards, a further acceleration can be observed through the use of technologies such as Big Data, artificial intelligence and the Internet of Things. These technologies enable ever faster processing of data and automated control of processes in real time.

A practical example of the impact of digitalisation on speeding up processes is online shopping. In the past, you had to go to a shop to buy products, which took time and effort. Today, you can order online with a few clicks and the desired product is often delivered the same day or within a few days.

Another example of an enormous acceleration of processes through digitalisation would be the sending of letters and emails. While sending a letter by post can take days or even weeks, an email reaches the recipient within seconds—an acceleration by a factor of 10,000 or more.

Digitalisation has created the opportunity to automate and speed up processes by replacing or complementing human labour with technology. This makes processes faster, more efficient and more cost-effective, which in turn benefits businesses and customers.

Digitalisation 4.0 goes one step further and refers to the integration of data, processes and systems throughout the entire value chain. Here, technologies such as artificial intelligence, the Internet of Things and Big Data are used to create a seamless, intelligent and optimised process chain.

In this chapter, we will take a closer look at digitalisation and Digitalisation 4.0 and examine their impact on companies, managers and knowledge workers. We will also discuss the challenges and opportunities of these developments and provide concrete recommendations for action for a successful digitalisation strategy.

2.3 Exponential Change

Digitisation means that processes and information are recorded, processed and stored electronically. As a result, processes can be carried out faster, more efficiently and with fewer errors. New possibilities arise for sharing, analysing and using information. Acceleration through digitalisation means that processes and decisions can be made faster, as information is available more quickly and communication channels become shorter.

This acceleration is making change in the economy and society exponential. Ever faster changing technologies and the resulting new opportunities and demands require constant adaptation and change. Companies need to act and react faster to remain competitive.

One example is the increasing automation and digitalisation of production processes. In the past, a lot of work had to be done manually, which took a lot of time and was prone to errors. With automation, these processes are carried out faster and more efficiently. As a result, products are manufactured faster and more cost-effectively and companies can respond more quickly to the needs of the market.

2.4 Effects and Requirements

Digitalisation has numerous impacts on society, the economy and technology. Here are some of them:

- **Automation:** Through the use of digital technologies such as robots and artificial intelligence, many manual and repetitive tasks are automated, leading to greater efficiency and productivity.
- **Changing workplaces:** As many tasks are automated, the requirements for jobs also change. New job profiles are emerging and skills are being weighted differently.
- **Globalisation:** Digital technologies enable companies to work from anywhere and tap into markets around the world.
- **New business models:** Digital technologies have changed the way companies can offer and sell products and services. The introduction of e-commerce and SaaS models are just a few examples.
- **Changing communication:** Digital technologies have changed the way we communicate. Social media and instant messaging apps have helped us communicate faster and easier.
- **Data security and data protection:** Increasing digitalisation has also led to new challenges in terms of data security and data protection. It is more important than ever to protect sensitive data.
- **Education:** Digitalisation also has an impact on education. New ways of acquiring and sharing knowledge are emerging, for example through online courses and virtual classrooms.
- **Societal changes:** Digitisation also has an impact on society by changing the way we live, work and interact. The social impact of digitalisation is not yet fully known, but it is clear that it has changed our society in many ways.

Summary

In this chapter, the different phases of digitalisation were explained and the effects of these developments on companies, managers and knowledge workers were discussed. It became clear that digitalisation has far-reaching effects on value creation processes, the demands on companies and employees as well as on society as a whole.

Digitalisation has led to an exponential change that poses new challenges for companies and at the same time offers new opportunities. Companies must adapt their business models and processes in order to remain competitive and take advantage of the opportunities of digitalisation. The manager as a central actor in the company must adapt his tasks and tools to meet these requirements.

For knowledge workers, digitalisation means a change in the requirements for their effectiveness and efficiency. Knowledge workers must be able to use new technologies and methods to make their work effective and ensure the success of the company.

In the next chapter, we will take a closer look at the knowledge worker as a central actor in the knowledge society and examine what requirements arise from this and how companies and managers can meet these requirements.

References

Handy, C. B. (1995). *The progress trap. Giving new meaning to the future*. Gabler.
Malik, F. (2019). *Führen, Leisten, Leben. Effective management for a new world*. Campus Verlag.

Online Sources

Management Blog: Management classics for those in a hurry (5) - The top ten management literature in a nutshell: Fredmund Malik "Führen Leisten Leben". https://blog.wiwo.de/management/2019/07/29/management-klassiker-fuer-eilige-5-die-top-ten-der-managementliteratur-auf-den-punkt-gebracht-fredmund-malik-fuehren-leisten-leben/, as of 27/03/2023.

3

The Knowledge Worker

3.1 Knowledge Work and Knowledge Workers

The most valuable capital of the twentieth century was its means of production. The most valuable capital of a twenty-first-century institution, whether private or non-profit, will be its knowledge workers and their productivity. (Drucker, 1999)

For Peter F. Drucker, knowledge work is an activity in which the employee has a deep understanding and extensive knowledge in a specific area to perform complex tasks. Unlike manual work, which is mostly standardised and repetitive, knowledge work often requires creative thinking, analytical judgement and problem-solving skills.

Knowledge work is also often team-oriented and requires close cooperation with other professionals. The work often takes place in a dynamic and fast-changing environment where knowledge workers need to continuously update their knowledge and skills to meet the demands.

Overall, for Peter F. Drucker, the ability to generate and use knowledge is a key factor for the success of knowledge workers and companies in today's economy.

In contrast to "normal" work, which is usually repeatable and thus predictable, knowledge work refers to creative activities based on individual knowledge, experience and judgement. It is characteristic of knowledge work that it is not always known in advance, but often only develops in the course of the work process. This makes it often more difficult to define and measure the success of knowledge work in advance than with "normal" work. In addition, knowledge work is usually more difficult to standardise and automate than "normal" work.

3.2 Tool

In today's knowledge society, knowledge work and knowledge workers play an increasingly important role. Unlike in the industrial society, where physical work was in the foreground, today it is mainly about processing information, solving problems and being creative. In the process, the demands on workers have increased enormously and place high demands on the mental system.

However, the limitations of our mental system are omnipresent and can lead to errors and limitations. Therefore, it is important to be aware of what defects of our thinking exist and how we can overcome them to make better decisions and perform more successful knowledge work. In this chapter, we will take a closer look at the role of the knowledge worker and the limitations of our mental system and present possible solutions for better knowledge work.

3.2.1 The Mental System

The mental system is the central tool of the knowledge worker. Unlike in industrial production, where the focus is on physical work, in knowledge work it is crucial to process information, solve problems and generate creative ideas. The knowledge worker's mental system is the instrument with which he or she accomplishes these tasks. It is composed of various elements, such as the working memory, which enables us to store and process information in the short term, and the long-term memory, in which all our knowledge and experiences are stored.

In addition, our ability to perceive, pay attention, concentrate and solve problems also plays an important role. However, the limitations of our mental system are omnipresent and can affect the effectiveness of our work. Errors can occur if, for example, we misinterpret information, allow ourselves to be influenced by our emotions or draw conclusions too quickly.

3.2.2 The Limitations of the Mental System

A knowledge worker is generally tasked with gathering and processing information and finding creative solutions to complex problems. Depending on the professional field, the work of a knowledge worker can look very different, but in general it is characterised by a high degree of autonomy, creativity and freedom of decision.

Therefore, it is crucial that the knowledge worker is aware of the limitations of his mental system and how he can overcome them to achieve better results.

In his book *Fast Thinking, Slow Thinking*, Daniel Kahneman describes a series of defects that can occur in our mental system.

A now classic example from the aforementioned book is as follows:

> **Example**
>
> Imagine you buy a racket and a ball and the total cost is 1.10 euros. The racket costs 1 euro more than the ball. How much does the ball cost? [Kahn12]
>
> In this example, our quick thinking (System 1) often intuitively jumps to the wrong answer: 10 cents. This is because our brain quickly grasps the difference of 1 euro and divides the cost in the simplest way: 1 euro for the bat and 10 cents for the ball. In fact, however, this is not the correct answer.

> To find the right answer, we need to use our slow thinking (System 2) to analyse the problem more thoroughly. Let us represent the information mathematically:
> Racket price = ball price + 1 Euro Total price = racket price + ball price
> Since the total price is 1.10 euros, we can write the equations as follows: Racket price = ball price + 1 Euro
> 1.10 Euro = racket price + ball price
> If we combine the two equations, we get: 1.10 Euro = (ball price + 1 Euro) + ball price
> To find the ball price, we solve the equation: 1.10 Euro - 1 Euro = 2 * ball price
> 0.10 Euro = 2 * ball price Ball price = 0.05 Euro

So the correct answer is 5 cents for the ball and 1.05 euros for the bat. This example shows how the representativeness heuristic and our quick thinking can often lead us to hasty, wrong conclusions.

Possible implications of Kahneman's defects for the work of a knowledge worker are:

- **Distortions in the perception of probabilities and risks:** A knowledge worker might tend to see probable events as improbable and improbable events as more probable than they actually are. This could lead him to make decisions based not on objective facts but on distorted assumptions.(Kahneman, 2012)
- **Overconfidence:** If a knowledge worker overestimates their skills and knowledge and relies too much on their intuition, they may make decisions that later turn out to be incorrect. Overconfidence can also lead to the knowledge worker not investing enough time and effort in preparation, which can have a negative impact on the quality of their work.
- **Availability heuristic:** If a knowledge worker relies on information that is readily available instead of conducting more comprehensive analyses, he might draw wrong conclusions and arrive at inaccurate results.
- **Influence of emotions on thinking:** Our emotions can influence our thinking and lead us to make decisions that are not rational. If a

knowledge worker is guided by their emotions instead of considering more objective factors, they could come to the wrong conclusions and decisions.
- **Confirmation bias:** If a knowledge worker prefers information that confirms their existing beliefs and biases rather than considering alternative views and opinions, they may be blind to facts and realities that contradict their view.
- **Framing effect:** The way a question or problem is presented can influence our decisions. A knowledge worker who is unable to evaluate the information they receive, regardless of how it is presented, could come to the wrong conclusion and make poor decisions.
- **Anchor heuristic:** If a knowledge worker "anchors" too much to certain information and makes decisions according to it instead of considering all the relevant facts, they might limit themselves and miss important information.

It is important that knowledge workers are aware of the defects in our mental system that can occur in their work and how they can overcome them to make better decisions and achieve more successful results. This includes techniques such as critical thinking, problem-solving skills, creative thought processes and decision-making based on objective facts and comprehensive analysis. Knowledge workers can also benefit from targeted training and the conscious application of methods and techniques to improve their skills and mental system.

Another important aspect is collaboration and communication with other knowledge workers. By collaborating and sharing ideas and perspectives, knowledge workers can improve their own work and develop a broader understanding of complex problems.

Overall, it is crucial that knowledge workers are aware of how the limitations of our mental system can affect their work in order to achieve better results and be more effective. By improving their skills and techniques to overcome these defects, knowledge workers can perform their work at the highest level and contribute to the advancement of society.

3.3 Change

For the knowledge worker, change means that the way they work and the way they use knowledge and information is continuously changing. The knowledge worker must be able to adapt quickly to new technologies, working methods and processes in order to remain productive and competitive. Change can occur for a variety of reasons, such as technological advances, changing customer requirements or new market conditions.

A knowledge worker can trigger change itself by finding innovative solutions to existing problems or identifying new business opportunities. For example, a knowledge worker may introduce a new technology or a new working model to increase efficiency and productivity or to create new business opportunities. By introducing such innovations, the knowledge worker can advance the company and advance his or her own career.

When change comes to the knowledge worker from the outside, he or she can respond by continuing education and acquiring new skills and knowledge. It is important that the knowledge worker is able to respond quickly to change and adapt to the demands of the new work environment. Here are some examples of how the knowledge worker can respond to change:

- **Continuous learning and training:** The knowledge worker should continuously learn and acquire new skills and knowledge to keep up with new technologies and working methods.
- **Agile working:** The knowledge worker should be able to react quickly to changes and be flexible to adapt quickly to new working conditions.
- **Innovative thinking:** The knowledge worker should be able to be creative and innovative to find new solutions to existing problems and move the company forward.
- **Collaboration and networking:** The knowledge worker should be able to collaborate with others and work in networks to share knowledge and experience and develop new ideas.

In summary, the knowledge worker must be able to adapt quickly to change and be flexible in order to succeed in a rapidly changing work environment. The knowledge worker can trigger change themselves by developing innovative solutions or identifying new business opportunities, or they can respond to change by continuing their education and acquiring new skills and knowledge.

3.4 Digitisation

The different phases of digitalisation have continuously changed the demands on knowledge workers. In the Digitisation 1.0 phase, mainly manual tasks were replaced by computers. Knowledge workers were usually experts in using these computers and often had technical backgrounds.

With the introduction of PCs in the Digitalisation 2.0 phase, computers became more affordable and more widely accessible. Knowledge workers now no longer necessarily needed to be technically skilled, but rather needed knowledge of how to use software applications.

With the introduction of the internet in the Digitalisation 3.0 phase, data and information became more accessible across organisational boundaries. Knowledge workers had to learn to deal with an increasingly globalised and networked working world and focus on processing data and information from different sources.

In the Digitalisation 4.0 phase, increasingly complex decisions are being made by computers with the introduction of artificial intelligence and machine learning. Knowledge workers must now be able to understand and use machines and algorithms to make better decisions. They also need to be able to focus on developing strategies and creative solutions as automated processes are increasingly taken over.

The defects of our mental system, as described by Daniel Kahneman, can affect our ability to make objective decisions and influence our performance as knowledge workers. Therefore, here is a general comparison of how digitalisation can influence these defects, both by mitigating and reinforcing them. By being aware of how digitalisation can influence our thought processes, we can improve our skills and techniques to make better informed decisions.

1. **Biases in the perception of probabilities and risks:** Digitisation can help ensure that knowledge workers have access to a wider range of data and information, which can help them support more informed decision-making and reduce potential biases in the perception of probabilities and risks.
2. **Overconfidence:** Digitalisation can increase the conviction and optimism of knowledge workers, as they can always be up to date through networking and communicating with others in real time. However, this can also lead to overconfidence, which can result in important information being overlooked or risks not being sufficiently considered.
3. **Availability heuristic:** Digitisation can contribute to knowledge workers reaching a decision quickly due to the availability of extensive amounts of data without taking enough time to conduct a careful analysis. It is important that knowledge workers are aware of what information is available and what information is missing in order to make an informed decision.
4. **Influence of emotions on thinking:** Digitalisation can contribute to knowledge workers being able to make decisions based on objective data and facts, rather than emotions or prejudices. At the same time, however, the influence of social media or other digital communication tools can also lead to knowledge workers being influenced by emotions that affect their decisions.
5. **Confirmation bias:** Digitisation can help knowledge workers to have access to a variety of opinions and perspectives, which can help them to challenge their own beliefs and consider alternative perspectives. At the same time, however, the use of filter bubbles and algorithms that work on the basis of user preferences can also lead to knowledge workers only being confronted with information that confirms their existing beliefs and prejudices.
6. **Framing effect:** Digitisation can contribute to knowledge workers having access to a wider range of information and being able to make decisions based on objective facts rather than biased or manipulated information. At the same time, however, algorithms or media can also influence the way information is presented, which can reinforce the framing effect.
7. **Anchor heuristics:** Digitisation can help knowledge workers have a broader range of data and information to make decisions, rather than

being "anchored" to specific data or numbers. At the same time, the use of dashboards that highlight certain metrics can lead to knowledge workers being too focused on those metrics and overlooking other important factors.

Overall, digitalisation can contribute to mitigating Kahneman's defects by facilitating access to more comprehensive data and information and allowing decisions to be made on the basis of objective facts. At the same time, however, digitalisation can also contribute to reinforcing some of the defects by leading to overconfidence or a bias in the presentation of information.

3.5 Requirements

The impact of digitalisation and acceleration on knowledge work is enormous. Knowledge workers need to constantly adapt to new challenges and changes to keep their competences and skills up to date. Traditional working methods and processes can no longer keep up to compete in this fast-paced world.

However, digitalisation also enables knowledge workers to find new ways and opportunities to do their work. By using new technologies such as artificial intelligence, big data and machine learning, they can optimise the way they work and gain new insights. But at the same time, they also need to learn how to best use and deploy these technologies to do their work effectively.

The combination of exponential change and digitalisation therefore requires a rethink of the way we acquire, process and use knowledge. Companies need to adapt their working methods and processes to make the most of the opportunities of digitalisation, and knowledge workers need to upgrade their skills and competences to keep pace with this change.

Change has always placed certain demands on the knowledge worker, such as

- Ability to learn quickly and adapt to new technologies and processes
- Ability to be creative and innovative and to find new solutions

- Ability to be flexible and adaptable and to adjust quickly to changes in work
- Ability to work effectively in teams and communicate via virtual communication channels
- Ability to deal with new technologies and information sources

Requirements resulting from digitalisation for the knowledge worker include:

- Digital competence and knowledge in the use of digital technologies and tools
- Ability to deal with Big Data and other digital information sources
- Ability to be creative and innovative and to develop digital solutions
- Ability to work in virtual teams and communicate via digital communication channels
- Ability to learn quickly and adapt to new technologies and processes

Summary

This chapter deals with the specific demands on the knowledge worker in a digitalised and networked world of work. Peter F. Drucker describes the importance of knowledge and knowledge work for companies and the role of the knowledge worker as a decisive factor for the success of a company. It also deals with the differences between the work of industrial workers and knowledge workers and the effectiveness and efficiency in knowledge work.

In addition, the effects of digitalisation on the demands on the knowledge worker are considered, especially with regard to the increasing complexity, uncertainty and fast pace in the world of work. This results in new demands on the competences and skills of the knowledge worker.

In this chapter, the mental defects according to Daniel Kahneman were also introduced. These defects refer to systematic errors in thinking that prevent us from deciding rationally and objectively.

The transition to the next chapter "The Manager" results from the fact that the knowledge worker is usually part of a company and is thus also influenced by the leadership and management of the company. The manager must therefore understand the special demands on the knowledge worker and create suitable framework conditions to promote the effectiveness and efficiency of knowledge work.

References

Drucker, P. F. (1974). *New management practice. Volume 1 - Tasks Volume 2 - Methods.* Econ-Verlag.

Drucker, P. F. (1999). *Management im 21. Jahrhundert.* ECON.

Kahneman, D. (2012). *Fast thinking, slow thinking.* Siedler Verlag.

Online Sources

Management Blog: Management classics for those in a hurry (5) - The top ten management literature in a nutshell: Fredmund Malik "Führen Leisten Leben". https://blog.wiwo.de/management/2019/07/29/management-klassiker-fuer-eilige-5-die-top-ten-der-managementliteratur-auf-den-punkt-gebracht-fredmund-malik-fuehren-leisten-leben/, as of 27/03/2023.

4

The Manager

The first is that management, that is the organ of leadership, direction and decision-making in our social institutions, and especially in business enterprises, is a generic function. (Drucker, 1974)

4.1 Role of the Manager

4.1.1 Tasks

Peter F. Drucker defined the tasks and methods of the manager in his book *The Practice of Management*. At the highest level of classification, he distinguishes between three tasks:

- **Company-related task:** The manager must ensure that the company is successful in the long term. This includes setting goals and strategies, organising the company's processes and monitoring performance and adapting to changes in the environment.
- **Employee-related task:** The manager is responsible for leading, developing and motivating employees. This includes hiring and firing

employees, training and developing skills, as well as monitoring performance and assessing employee performance.
- **Role related to society and the environment:** The manager is also responsible for the company's impact on society and the environment. This includes complying with laws and regulations, implementing environmentally friendly practices and creating positive relationships with the community and other stakeholders.

These tasks are closely interrelated and require different skills and knowledge to be successful. The manager must be able to balance the different tasks and delegate effectively to ensure that all aspects of the business are successful.

The employee-related task is the subject of this book when it comes specifically to the knowledge worker. Let us therefore take a closer look at this task, which is about effectiveness and efficiency:

There is a crucial difference in the effectiveness of the knowledge worker compared to the industrial worker: The effectiveness of the industrial worker refers to the execution of the task according to the instructions and standards of the company. The industrial worker should do his job as effectively as possible in order to generate the greatest possible benefit for the company.

In contrast, the effectiveness of the knowledge worker refers to the achievement of the goals and outcomes that are critical to the success of the organisation. The knowledge worker must do his or her work in a way that generates the greatest possible benefit for the company and focuses on the important goals and results. The focus is thus on achieving the goals and not on performing according to predefined standards.

The employee-related task of the manager according to Drucker involves the effective leadership and development of the employees in the company. This involves creating a suitable organisational structure and working environment that enables knowledge workers to realise their full potential. The manager must ensure that employees are sufficiently promoted and that their skills are optimally utilised.

In order to lead staff effectively, managers must also have good communication and empathy skills. They must be able to understand and respond appropriately to the needs and expectations of their employees.

An important aspect here is also the creation of a positive corporate culture that promotes open and cooperative collaboration.

In addition, it is the manager's task to motivate the employees for continuous training and innovation. Fostering the skills and creativity of employees is an important factor for the success of the company in the age of digitalisation. Effective innovation management that harnesses the ideas and potential of employees can provide a decisive competitive advantage and make the company fit for the future.

4.1.2 Tools

Drucker names three tools of the manager: the goal, planning and communication. In his book *The Effective Executive* he structures them in a more differentiated way as follows:

1. **Meetings:** Meetings are a manager's tool to gather and share information and make decisions. They allow ideas to be discussed and problems to be solved.
2. **Reports and written communication:** Reports and written communication are an important part of the manager's work to communicate information to others and to coordinate the work of the company.
3. **Job design and assignment control:** Job design and assignment control refer to the design of work processes and the assignment of tasks to employees. A well-designed work environment can improve employee performance.
4. **Personal work methodology:** Personal work methodology refers to the way a manager works. It is about how a manager plans and organises his or her time to do the job effectively.
5. **Budget and budgeting:** Budget and budgeting refer to the financial planning of the enterprise. It is about using the company's resources effectively to achieve the company's goals.
6. **Performance appraisal:** Performance appraisal refers to the evaluation of employees' performance. It is about finding out how well an employee has done their tasks and how they can improve their work.

7. **Systematic waste removal:** Systematic waste removal refers to the elimination of ineffective and unproductive workflows and processes. It is about ensuring that the company only carries out the necessary activities and does not waste unnecessary resources.

4.1.3 Principles

Peter Drucker has formulated a number of principles and advice for managers throughout his career. Here are some key principles Drucker proposed for effective management:

- **Management by objectives (MBO):** Set clear, measurable goals and direct the efforts of all staff towards these goals.
- **Focus on strengths: Focus on** employees' strengths and use them to increase performance and productivity. Weaknesses should be minimised but not the main focus.
- **Time management:** Analyse and optimise the use of your time and the time of your employees to be more productive and efficient.
- **Effective decision-making:** Make decisions based on facts, data and sound analysis and look for the best solutions for the organisation.
- **Delegation and empowerment:** Promote autonomy and responsibility by empowering employees to make decisions and shape their own work.
- **Communication and cooperation:** Encourage open communication, promote teamwork and create an atmosphere of trust and mutual respect.
- **Innovation and continuous improvement:** Encourage innovation and creative thinking and promote a culture of continuous improvement to ensure growth and competitiveness.
- **Focus on results:** Focus on achieving results and measure performance based on these results, not just on activities and processes.
- **Ethics and social responsibility:** Pay attention to ethical behaviour and social responsibility, both within the organisation and in relation to external stakeholders.

These principles provide a framework for developing effective management practices and enhancing the performance of managers and their teams.

4.1.4 Knowledge Workers

The manager is often a knowledge worker in today's working world, as he is usually in a position where he has to make decisions based on knowledge. His work consists of collecting, analysing and evaluating information in order to then take appropriate action. The manager is thus a knowledge worker who primarily does mental work and draws on his knowledge and experience to solve problems and make decisions.

Another important aspect of managers' work as knowledge workers is communication. As they usually have responsibility for other employees, they also need to be able to share their knowledge and experience and support their employees in solving problems. In this context, the manager's ability to collaborate and create synergies with others is also crucial. The manager as a knowledge worker must therefore not only have a variety of skills and knowledge themselves but also be able to use and share these skills and knowledge effectively in order to be successful.

For the manager, possible defects according to Kahneman that could occur in his tasks are:

- **Planning:** The availability heuristic may play a role in planning, as the manager may tend to make decisions based on information that is readily available rather than more careful analysis. The representativeness heuristic may also play a role if the manager uses similar past experiences or patterns as a model for the future.
- **Organisation:** The framing effect could play a role here if the manager makes decisions based on the way information is presented instead of being more objective. Also the influence of emotions on thinking could lead to the manager making decisions based on personal preferences or prejudices.
- **Motivation:** The confirmation bias could play a role if the manager prefers information that confirms his or her existing beliefs and biases

instead of seeking more objective information. The influence of emotions on thinking may also play a role here if the manager makes decisions based on emotions rather than objective facts.
- **Control:** The anchor effect could play a role here, if the manager "anchors" himself too much to certain information or numbers and makes decisions according to them instead of considering all the facts. The influence of emotions on thinking could also lead to the manager making decisions based on personal likes or dislikes.

Overall, it is important for the manager to be aware of the limitations of our mental system that can occur in any task and how to overcome them in order to make better decisions and be more effective. This also includes regularly questioning oneself in a self-critical way and considering alternative views and opinions.

4.2 Change

Change is one of the fundamental challenges that managers face. A manager is responsible for ensuring that a company is able to adapt to changes in the environment and seize new opportunities. This includes the ability to manage change within the company. The manager must ensure that all employees are prepared for change and have the necessary skills and resources to manage change. It is important that the manager has a clear vision for the company and communicates this vision. Only then can the whole company work in a common direction and successfully manage change. The manager must also be able to identify risks and opportunities and make decisions that secure the future of the company.

An example of change and the challenges it poses for the manager is the changeover to a new production method. Not only do the technical processes have to be adapted but also the employees have to be trained accordingly and adapt to the changes. The manager has to make sure that everyone is involved and that the changeover goes smoothly.

As Warren Bennis said: "*Management is doing things right; leadership is doing the right things*" [Spri23]. This quote underlines the importance of the leader not only doing the processes right but also making the decisions that lead in the right direction. In times of change, this leadership task becomes even more important as it points the way for the company and sets the course for a successful future.

4.3 Digitisation

The individual phases of digitalisation have significantly changed the demands on the manager. While in the early years of digitalisation the manager's focus was primarily on the introduction and implementation of IT systems, new requirements have emerged with the later phases. Today, for example, managers are in demand who are familiar with digitisation and the associated technological developments and are able to recognise and react to opportunities and risks for the company.

Furthermore, digitalisation also requires a new understanding of leadership and collaboration. Agility and flexibility are more important than ever in today's world in order to react quickly to change and drive innovation. The manager must therefore be able to adapt the way of working in the company to the new circumstances and promote a culture of collaboration and knowledge sharing. A stronger focus on the customer and their needs is also essential in the digital world.

Through the different phases of digitalisation, the role of the manager has changed significantly. In the first phase of digitalisation (Digitalisation 1.0), the manager's focus was mainly on optimising production processes. In the second phase (Digitalisation 2.0), above all the possibilities of information processing through computers were recognised and used. The manager now had to pay more attention to the IT infrastructure and systems in order to ensure efficient operations.

With the third phase (Digitalisation 3.0), the role of the manager was expanded again, as the internet and the associated new communication and sales channels were now also used. The manager now had to keep an eye not only on the IT systems but also on the company's online presence and strategy.

In the current phase of digitalisation (Digitalisation 4.0), the manager faces new challenges. Due to the progressive networking of machines and systems as well as the possibilities of Big Data and artificial intelligence, the manager must be able to make data-driven decisions and accompany the company on the path to Industry 4.0.

Let's now take a look at the possible effects of digitalisation on the manager's tasks, taking into account the findings of Daniel Kahneman:

1. **Planning:** Digitisation can facilitate access to more comprehensive and accurate data, which can help reduce the influence of the availability heuristic. At the same time, however, algorithms or dashboards can also increase the influence of the anchor effect by putting the manager's focus on certain metrics that can constrain planning and decision-making.
2. **Organisation:** Digitisation can help support better organisation and structuring of data and information, which can help reduce the framing effect. At the same time, however, the use of algorithms and dashboards or the automation of processes can also lead to the manager overlooking important information and factors or the need for human judgement and creativity.
3. **Motivation:** Digitalisation can help to reduce the manager's workload through automated processes, which creates time and space for creativity and innovation. At the same time, however, the influence of emotions can also be increased through the use of social media platforms and the increased speed and intensity of communication, which can lead to the manager making decisions based on emotional reactions rather than objective facts.
4. **Control:** Digitisation can help managers have a better understanding of team and staff performance by giving them access to more comprehensive data. At the same time, however, dashboards and algorithms can also increase the influence of the anchor effect by putting the manager's focus on certain metrics that may not reflect overall performance.

Overall, digitalisation can contribute to making the manager's tasks easier by facilitating access to more comprehensive data and information and by enabling decisions to be made on the basis of objective facts. At the same time, however, digitalisation can also contribute to the amplification of some defects by placing the manager's focus on certain metrics or data and overlooking important information or overlooking human judgement and creativity.

4.4 Requirements

This results in, among other things, the following requirements for managers in general:

- Understanding of technological developments and their impact on the company and the market
- Ability to manage change effectively and steer transformation processes
- Ability to make quick decisions based on data and analysis
- Ability to innovate and find new solutions to drive the business forward
- Ability to respond to rapidly changing market conditions

When looking at change through digitalisation, some of the above requirements would still be relevant, while others may become less important or be replaced by other requirements, with the ability to effectively manage change and steer digital transformation processes probably being the most central requirement.

> **Summary**
>
> In this chapter we looked at what tasks and tools a manager needs to be successful. We have seen that a manager must not only be an effective communicator but also be able to develop and motivate his or her staff. Furthermore, we have seen that a manager is also a knowledge worker who must be able to solve complex problems and think strategically.
>
> With regard to digitalisation and exponential change, the basic tasks of the manager do not change. Goal setting and planning, organisation and structuring, human resource management, control and monitoring, as well as innovation and change management remain crucial tasks that a manager must master.
>
> However, digitalisation and exponential change have changed the methods a manager can use to accomplish these tasks. Technology has fundamentally changed the way companies and managers work. Modern

technologies such as cloud computing, big data, artificial intelligence and the Internet of Things offer new possibilities for automating business processes and analysing data. This enables managers to make informed decisions and react quickly to changes.

Another important factor in the digital world is the way people collaborate and communicate. Virtual teams and global collaboration have become more common in the digital world and pose new challenges to management practice.

Overall, the fundamental role of the manager in the digital world remains unchanged, but managers need to adapt their methods to succeed in the fast-moving digital landscape. The ability to use technology and find innovative solutions are important factors to be successful.

It is also important to emphasise that a manager never acts alone, but always within a company. Therefore, in the next chapter, "The Company", we need to look at how the demands on companies are changing due to exponential change and digitalisation and how companies can adapt to this. In doing so, we will also see what role the manager plays within a company and how he can deal with these changes.

Reference

Drucker, P. F. (1974). *New management practice. Volume 1 - Tasks Volume 2 - Methods*. Econ-Verlag.

Online Sources

Management Blog: Management classics for those in a hurry (5) - The top ten management literature in a nutshell: Fredmund Malik "Führen Leisten Leben". https://blog.wiwo.de/management/2019/07/29/management-klassiker-fuer-eilige-5-die-top-ten-der-managementliteratur-auf-den-punkt-gebracht-fredmund-malik-fuehren-leisten-leben/, as of 27/03/2023.

SpringerLink: "Managers do things right. Leaders do the right thing". https://link.springer.com/chapter/10.1007/978-3-322-82771-5_7, as of 26/03/2023.

5

The Company

5.1 Purpose

According to Peter F. Drucker, the purpose of a company is to create customer value. In his words:

> There is only one valid purpose for a business: to create customers. (Drucker, 1998)

He believes that the purpose of a company is not just to make profits. In his book *Management: Tasks, Responsibilities, Practices*, he emphasises that companies can only exist because they satisfy a need among their customers. It is therefore their task to provide benefits to customers and thus to fulfil societal needs. A company is therefore part of society and has a social responsibility.

Drucker sees it as essential that a company has a clear mission and knows its goals and the expectations of its customers. The company must act accordingly to meet the needs of its customers and thus be economically successful. In doing so, the company should also act in accordance with social values and norms in order to fulfil its social responsibility.

Drucker was an advocate of the social market economy and saw companies as an important part of society that should not only focus on their own profit but also work for the common good.

5.2 Change

Peter F. Drucker distinguishes the change that companies have to face into two categories: change outside the company and change inside the company. Change outside the company refers to the changes in society, the economy and technology that can influence the company but cannot be directly controlled by it. This involves, for example, changes in the market environment, new technologies and changes in societal values.

Change within the company, on the other hand, refers to the changes that the company itself can initiate and control. This involves changes in organisational structure, corporate culture, work processes and management structures. These changes may be necessary in order to be able to react to change outside the company, but also to keep the company itself fit for the future and to increase its competitiveness.

In general, change in a company can be divided into three phases:

- **Foundation phase:** In this phase, the company is in the foundation and set-up phase. The main focus is on developing a business idea and establishing the company in the market. In this phase, the focus is on the survival of the company.
- **Growth phase:** In this phase the company grows and establishes itself in the market. The company focuses on improving and expanding its products or services and gaining new customers. The goal is to gain market share and consolidate its position in the market.
- **Maturity phase:** In this phase, the company has established its position in the market and focuses on optimising its products or services, reducing costs and increasing efficiency. The company sets itself the goal of maintaining its market share and remaining profitable in the long term.

Digitalisation has accelerated the pace of change in these phases and companies have to adapt ever faster to changing market conditions. It is therefore important that companies remain agile and continuously adapt their strategies and processes.

Drucker also distinguishes between incremental change and disruptive change. Incremental change is a gradual process in which an organisation optimises its existing structures and processes to work more efficiently and improve the quality of its products or services. Disruptive change, on the other hand, refers to profound changes that can shake the foundation of a company by creating new technologies, market conditions or business models that can render the company's existing business practices and products obsolete.

Drucker emphasises that it is crucial for companies to prepare for disruptive change by remaining open to change and regularly rethinking their business models. He urges companies to constantly question themselves and face the challenges of change in order to be successful in the long term.

Digitalisation is bringing exponential change that is very different from previous changes in the world of work. Digitalisation is changing not only the way we work but also the speed and complexity of our work. The change is not linear, but is increasing at an ever faster pace. Companies need to adapt to the fact that they have to continuously adapt in order to remain competitive. It is about developing the ability to respond quickly to change while remaining agile and innovative. Change is not only about technology but also about the way people work and how companies are organised.

5.3 Digitisation

Digitisation 1.0 was mainly about automating individual processes within a company and thus increasing efficiency. Digitalisation 2.0 brought the personal computer and with it the possibility for knowledge workers to do their work directly on the computer. This led to more flexibility and mobility in work, but also to new demands on IT security and data management.

Digitalisation 3.0 with the emergence of the World Wide Web enabled the global networking of companies and people, which led to a further acceleration of business processes. Companies had to adjust to a faster responsiveness and adaptation to new technologies.

In Digitalisation 4.0, the boundaries between the physical and digital worlds are blurring and the aim is to digitalise companies as a whole, focusing on comprehensive networking and automation of processes. This requires a high degree of flexibility and agility as well as the ability to process and make sense of large amounts of data.

The phases of digitalisation have changed the way companies can achieve their purpose. In Digitalisations 1.0 and 2.0, the focus was on automating processes and increasing efficiency. Companies could now complete more tasks faster and with fewer workers, which ultimately led to cost savings and higher profits. Digitisation 3.0 emphasised the importance of customer interaction, as companies were now able to reach their customers directly via the internet. The focus was on improving the customer experience and building stronger customer loyalty.

With Digitalisation 4.0, the purpose of business has changed again. Now it is about maximising customer value through personalised offers and tailored solutions. Through the use of Big Data and artificial intelligence, companies are able to collect and analyse data on customer behaviour and preferences in order to adapt their offers and business models. The focus is not only on maximising efficiency but also on creating value for customers and society as a whole.

5.3.1 Innovation Management

Digitalisation can have a significant impact on a company's innovation management. Digitalisation can give rise to new technologies, processes and business models that enable or even require innovation. Companies must be able to react quickly to changes in the market and develop innovative solutions in order to remain competitive.

An important aspect of innovation management in the context of digitalisation is the ability to use and analyse data. By analysing data, companies can identify trends and optimise processes, which in turn can lead to innovations. Furthermore, digital technologies such as artificial intelligence and machine learning can support the development of innovative products and services.

Digitalisation can influence innovation through combination by facilitating access to information and technologies and thus creating the possibility to combine them. Digitalisation enables companies to collect and evaluate information about customers, products and markets more quickly and easily. This data can then be used to develop new products and services or improve existing ones. By combining technologies and innovations, companies can open up new business models and become more competitive. Digitalisation can therefore help companies to drive and implement innovations faster and more effectively.

Innovation management also plays an important role in the digitalisation of business models.

5.3.2 Business Model

Companies must be able to rethink their existing business models and develop new digital business models to respond to changing market conditions and customer needs. Here, an agile and flexible innovation culture is of great importance in order to be able to react quickly to new requirements.

Digitalisation can significantly influence or even revolutionise a company's business model. By enabling products and services to be produced, offered and marketed more quickly and efficiently. New technologies and digital platforms can make it easier for companies to develop innovative business models and better meet customers' needs. The possibilities for data analysis and processing can also help to optimise the value chain and open up new business areas. It is therefore important that companies closely analyse the impact of digitalisation on their business model and make adjustments where necessary to remain competitive in the long term.

5.4 Exponential Change

Exponential change does matter not only for start-ups but also for established companies. In fact, it is even more important for established companies to understand and use exponential change in order to remain competitive and not be displaced by disruptive innovations.

Established companies often have more resources and experience to take advantage of the opportunities of digitalisation and exponential change and can build on existing customer relationships and brand awareness. However, they must also be prepared to question and adapt their existing processes, structures and ways of thinking in order to successfully manage the change.

In order to unleash the exponential potential of a company, there are various approaches that are becoming increasingly important in the face of advancing digitalisation:

- **Benefits of Big Data:** By analysing large amounts of data, the company can gain valuable insights and react quickly and effectively to market changes based on them.
- **Agility and flexibility:** Companies should be able to react quickly to changes in the market and adapt to new circumstances. This requires an agile and flexible organisation that can adapt to changes quickly and effectively.
- **Innovation:** To remain competitive, a company must constantly develop new ideas and innovations. In doing so, the company should be open to change and willing to take risks in order to develop new business opportunities.
- **Collaboration:** Close collaboration within the company and with external partners and customers can help to increase the company's innovative strength and efficiency.
- **Leadership:** Clear leadership and strategy is crucial to unleash the exponential potential of the company. Leaders should clearly communicate the company's vision and motivate employees to work together to achieve it.

Overall, it is important for companies to constantly evolve and adapt to changing market conditions in order to realise their exponential potential. This requires a culture of change and innovation as well as clear leadership and strategy.

5.5 Requirements

This results in, among other things, the following requirements for companies in general:

- Adaptability to a rapidly changing world
- Developing an agile corporate culture that promotes continuous change
- Ability to react quickly to changes in technology, the economy and society
- Willingness to take risks and develop innovative business models
- Protection of data and security of systems and processes

Looking at the transformation through digitalisation, some of the above requirements would still be relevant, while others may become less important or be replaced by other requirements. Here are some examples:

- Flexibility and adaptability to changes in technology and market conditions
- Investing in new technologies and infrastructure to remain competitive
- Agility and the ability to innovate in order to respond to rapidly changing market conditions
- Protection of data and security of systems and processes
- Development of a digital strategy and integration of digital technologies into the business models

> **Summary**
>
> This chapter deals with the challenges and demands that digitalisation and exponential change place on companies.
> Peter F. Drucker describes the three main tasks of management, which are to ensure economic performance, labour productivity and job satisfaction, as well as social impact and social responsibility.
> The knowledge worker, as a central resource in the organisation, requires an effective and efficient way of working and paying special attention to his or her job satisfaction. Various tools and principles for effective leadership are described that are relevant to the manager's task performance.
> In the context of digitalisation and exponential change, companies must adapt their business models and innovation management processes to remain competitive. The increasing importance of data and information also places new demands on data management and data security.

References

Drucker, P. F. (1974). *New management practice. Volume 1 - Tasks Volume 2 - Methods*. Econ-Verlag.

Drucker, P. F. (1998). *The practice of management. A guide to management tasks in the modern economy*. ECON.

Online Sources

Management Blog: Management classics for those in a hurry (5) - The top ten management literature in a nutshell: Fredmund Malik "Führen Leisten Leben". https://blog.wiwo.de/management/2019/07/29/management-klassiker-fuer-eilige-5-die-top-ten-der-managementliteratur-auf-den-punkt-gebracht-fredmund-malik-fuehren-leisten-leben/, as of 27/03/2023.

Part II

Collective Intelligence as a System 3

What really matters is not so much what each individual knows, but rather what we construct together by working together.—[Lévy97]

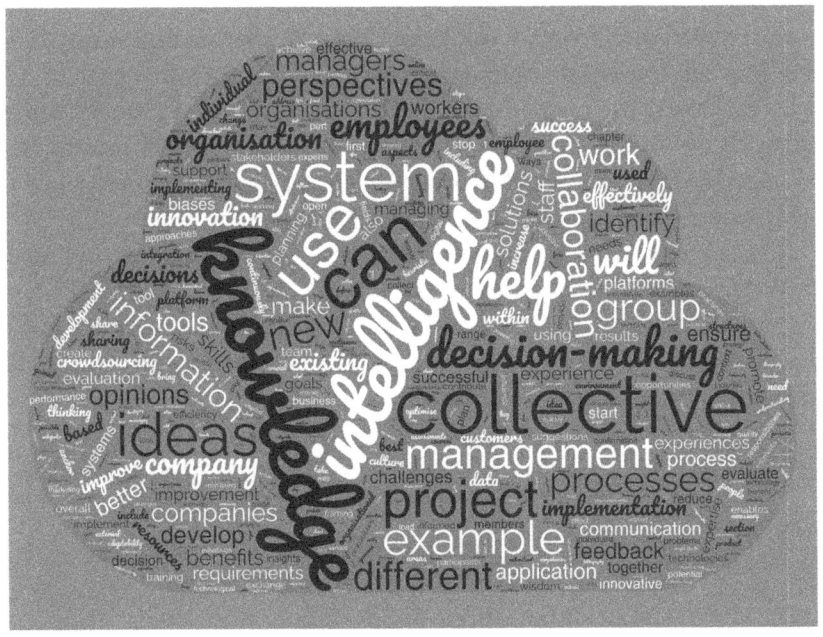

1.1 Outlook on Part II

In Part II of this book, we will look at a key tool that can help knowledge workers, managers and companies to cope with the increased demands and challenges in an increasingly digitalised and connected world: collective intelligence, which we call System 3.

First, in Chap. 6, System 3, we will introduce and define what is meant by collective intelligence. We will discuss the differentiation from other forms of intelligence and show various fields of application in which collective intelligence has been successfully used. Examples of successful implementations will also be presented to illustrate the practical relevance of this tool.

In Chap. 7 we will explore the benefits of System 3 for different stakeholders, including knowledge workers, managers and companies. We will discuss how collective intelligence can help address the needs identified in Part I and what the benefits are.

Chapter 8 will focus on the concrete application of System 3. We will explain the requirements for implementing collective intelligence systems and give step-by-step instructions on how to carry out a first project. We will also look at the evaluation and use of the results and present further examples of the successful use of System 3. Finally, we will present best practices and success factors for implementing collective intelligence in your own context and offer a checklist to facilitate the process.

By the end of Part II, you will have gained a deep understanding of collective intelligence as a tool to address the challenges of digital transformation. This knowledge will help you make informed decisions about the use of System 3 in your organisation and pave the way for a successful integration of collective intelligence.

6

Presentation of System 3: The Concept of Collective Intelligence

6.1 Definition

Kenneth Blanchard is credited with the quote: "None of us is as smart as all of us put together". This aptly sums up the essence of collective intelligence, regardless of whether Blanchard actually made this quote verbatim.

In Part 2 of this book, we will therefore take an in-depth look at the concept of collective intelligence, which we refer to as System 3 (cf. Fig. 6.1). At a time when digitalisation and networking are becoming increasingly important, collective intelligence is becoming a crucial factor in overcoming the diverse challenges and demands placed on knowledge workers, managers and companies. We will discuss the basics of System 3, highlight its importance and possible applications in different contexts and discuss how collective intelligence can be used to make better decisions, drive innovation and ultimately ensure the success of organisations in the digital era.

Collective intelligence is the ability of a group of individuals to work together, share knowledge and jointly solve problems or make decisions that go beyond what an individual could achieve alone. This form of

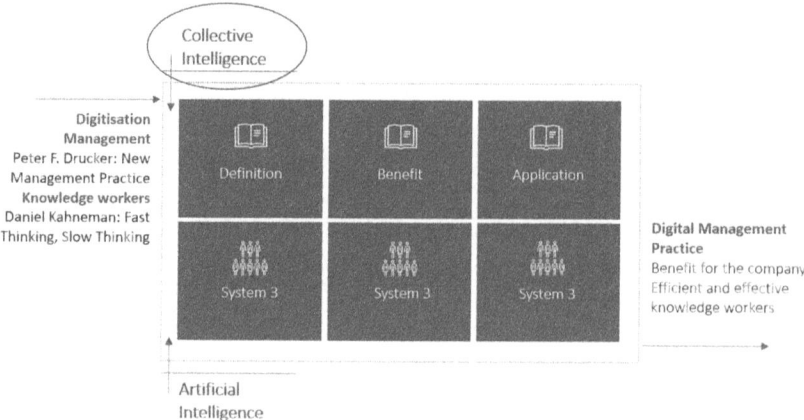

Fig. 6.1 Definition, benefits and application of collective intelligence as a System 3

intelligence comes from combining the individual skills, experiences and perspectives of group members, enabling them to harness synergies and develop innovative solutions to complex issues.

System 3 is based on the idea that the collective intelligence of a group is generally higher than the sum of the intelligences of its individual members. This is because collaboration and the exchange of knowledge and ideas expand the group's cognitive resources and generate new perspectives and approaches to solutions that might not have occurred to an individual member.

Collective intelligence can be used in different contexts, for example in organisations, teams, networks and online-based communities. It can emerge in both formal and informal structures and is fostered by factors such as open communication, trust, diversity and shared purpose. In the digital era, System 3 plays an increasingly important role as technologies such as the internet and social media enable the networking and sharing of knowledge and ideas on a global scale, supporting the emergence of collective intelligence.

A classic example is the story of Sir Francis Galton and the bull weight estimate, which is often cited as a classic example of collective intelligence. The story dates back to 1906, when the British statistician and scientist Sir Francis Galton made an interesting observation at a cattle market (folk festival).

6 Presentation of System 3: The Concept of Collective Intelligence

At this festival, there was a competition in which participants had to estimate the weight of a slaughtered and gutted bull. Around 800 people, including experts and lay people, took part in the competition and gave their estimates. After the contest was over, Galton analysed the estimates and found that the average estimate of the participants was amazingly accurate—only one pound away from the actual weight of the bull.

This example illustrates the concept of collective intelligence. Although the individual estimates of the participants varied and some of them were far from the actual number, the combination of their estimates led to an accurate prediction. The collective wisdom of the group surpassed the expertise of the individuals, and the aggregate intelligence of the crowd produced a more accurate result than most individuals could achieve.

Another example of the application of collective intelligence is the online encyclopaedia Wikipedia. Wikipedia is a collaborative project where thousands of volunteers from all over the world share their knowledge and expertise to jointly create a comprehensive and freely accessible source of information. Anyone can create, edit or expand articles, and the quality and accuracy of the content is continuously improved through community collaboration.

The collective intelligence of the Wikipedia community makes it possible to cover a wide range of topics that might not be included in traditional encyclopaedias or would have limited coverage. In addition, information can be updated quickly to reflect new developments and insights. The success of Wikipedia shows how collaboration and the exchange of knowledge and ideas in a networked community can help create a powerful and dynamic knowledge resource based on the collective intelligence of its members.

6.2 Delimitation

Collective intelligence differs from other tools and approaches in some key characteristics. Here are some delimitations to collective intelligence compared to other tools:

- **Individual versus collective intelligence:** While individual intelligence is based on the skills, knowledge and experience of an individual, collective intelligence is based on cooperation and knowledge sharing within a group. Collective intelligence goes beyond the sum of individual intelligences and enables the group to solve more complex problems.

- **Hierarchical versus decentralised decision-making:** In traditional, hierarchical organisations, decisions are often made by a single leader or a small group of leaders. Collective intelligence, on the other hand, relies on decentralised decision-making, where all members of a group contribute their ideas, opinions and expertise and work together to find solutions.
- **Closed versus open systems:** Collective intelligence can emerge in open systems where information and knowledge are freely shared and discussed. This is in contrast to closed systems where knowledge and information only circulate within a particular group or organisation and access to external knowledge is limited.
- **Fixed versus flexible structures:** In contrast to fixed structures that prevail in many organisations, collective intelligence initiatives can have flexible and adaptive structures that facilitate the exchange of knowledge and ideas and can respond more quickly to change.
- **Competition versus collaboration:** While many traditional tools are based on competition and individual performance, collective intelligence promotes collaboration, mutual support and shared learning.

Overall, collective intelligence is characterised by a greater emphasis on collaboration, openness, decentralisation and flexibility, compared to traditional tools and approaches that are often based on individual skills, hierarchical structures and closed systems.

6.3 Fields of Application

Collective intelligence is used in many different areas and fields of application. Here are some examples of fields of application of collective intelligence:

- **Knowledge management:** In organisations and companies, collective intelligence can help to collect, organise and use the knowledge and experience of employees to make better decisions and solve problems more efficiently.
- **Open innovation:** Collective intelligence can be used to capture innovative ideas and solutions from a wide range of stakeholders, including customers, suppliers and the general public, and incorporate them into the innovation process.
- **Online communities and social networks:** In online platforms such as Wikipedia, Reddit or Stack Overflow, users contribute their knowledge and expertise to jointly answer questions, share information and solve problems.
- **Crowdsourcing and crowd-funding:** Collective intelligence can be used to mobilise ideas, resources and capital from large numbers of people to support projects and initiatives that might not otherwise be realised.
- **Decision-making and forecasting:** Group decisions based on collective intelligence can in many cases lead to better outcomes than individual decisions. Moreover, collective forecasts, such as those made by Prediction Markets, can often be more accurate than individual predictions.
- **Crisis management and disaster relief:** Collective intelligence can help to coordinate information and resources effectively in emergency situations and respond more quickly to crises.
- **Environmental protection and sustainability:** Through collaboration between experts, organisations and the public, collective intelligence approaches can help identify environmental problems, develop solutions and promote sustainable behaviours.
- **Education and learning:** Collective intelligence can be used to promote shared learning and the exchange of knowledge and experiences in educational institutions and online platforms.

These examples show that collective intelligence can be used in many different areas and contexts to achieve better results, drive innovation and promote collaboration and the sharing of knowledge and resources.

The fields of application of collective intelligence show that it is an extremely valuable tool in various fields. In the context of knowledge work and digitalisation, collective intelligence, referred to as System 3, can play a crucial role in helping organisations address the challenges and opportunities arising from the rapid spread of digital technologies.

- **Accelerating knowledge work:** By fostering collaboration and knowledge sharing among knowledge workers, organisations can increase the efficiency and quality of their work and respond more quickly to changes in the market and technological environment.
- **Increase innovation:** The use of System 3 can help generate new ideas and solutions as knowledge workers share their expertise and perspectives. This collaborative innovation can help organisations stay competitive and excel in the digital economy.
- **Effective decision-making:** Collective intelligence can help ensure that decisions are made on a broader knowledge base and benefit from the expertise and experience of the whole organisation. This can lead to more informed decisions that help the organisation meet the challenges of digitalisation.
- **Adaptability and agility:** By using System 3, organisations can become more flexible, adaptable and responsive to the ever-changing demands of the digital economy. The ability to respond quickly to change and develop new solutions is critical in today's fast-paced world.
- **Talent management and employee retention:** By harnessing and nurturing the collective intelligence of their employees, organisations can achieve greater retention and motivation among employees, who feel valued and engaged because their opinions and ideas are taken into account.

Overall, the use of collective intelligence as System 3 in the context of knowledge work and digitalisation can help organisations better respond to the challenges and opportunities arising from the ever-evolving digital landscape. System 3 enables organisations to harness the collective wisdom and skills of their knowledge workers to increase their efficiency, innovation and adaptability.

6 Presentation of System 3: The Concept of Collective Intelligence

Summary

In this chapter, System 3, collective intelligence, was introduced and defined. The differentiation from other tools and the various fields of application of collective intelligence were outlined. The reference to its use as System 3 in the context of knowledge work and digitalisation was explained, showing the advantages and opportunities that arise from the application of collective intelligence in organisations.

Accelerating knowledge work, increasing innovation, effective decision-making, adaptability and agility as well as talent management and employee retention were highlighted as key aspects that can be supported and promoted by the use of System 3 in a digitalised world.

Reference

Lévy, P. (1997). *Collective intelligence. Mankind's emerging world in cyberspace.* Plenum Trade.

7

Benefits of System 3: The Collective Intelligence

7.1 Benefits for the Knowledge Worker

7.1.1 Distortions in Perception

Collective intelligence can help deal with biases in the perception of probabilities and risks by drawing on the cognitive resources and perspectives of a group of people. Here are some ways System 3 can help:

- **Diversity of perspectives:** By bringing together a group of people with different backgrounds, expertise and ways of thinking, collective intelligence can offset the effects of individual biases. The group can bring different perspectives on probabilities and risks, reducing the likelihood that individuals will remain trapped in their own biases.
- **Group decision-making:** Collective intelligence can improve the decision-making process by taking into account different opinions and assessments. Group decision-making can lead participants to question and reconsider their own assumptions, resulting in a more realistic assessment of probabilities and risks.

- **Aggregation of estimates:** One method of using collective intelligence to improve the perception of probabilities and risks is the aggregation of estimates from a group of people. The so-called wisdom of crowds states that the average estimate of a group is in many cases more accurate than the estimates of individual experts.
- **Use of feedback and learning processes:** Collective intelligence can also help knowledge workers learn from the experiences and insights of others. By sharing feedback and experiences, group members can rethink and adjust their own perceptions of probabilities and risks.
- **Technology support:** Modern technologies such as collaborative platforms and decision support tools can foster the collective intelligence of a group. These tools can help knowledge workers share, compare and aggregate their assessments of probabilities and risks to develop a better overall understanding.

Overall, System 3, collective intelligence, can help mitigate biases in the perception of probabilities and risks by harnessing and combining the strengths and perspectives of a group of people. This can lead to more informed and objective decisions that are less prone to cognitive biases.

7.1.2 Overconfidence

> Under the right circumstances, groups are remarkably intelligent—and often smarter than the smartest in their midst. —James Surowiecki (Surowiecki, 2007)

Collective intelligence can help reduce overconfidence among knowledge workers by incorporating different perspectives, experiences and opinions into decision-making processes. When a knowledge worker relies on collective wisdom in a group, it can lead to putting their personal conviction of their skills and knowledge into perspective.

7 Benefits of System 3: The Collective Intelligence

> **Example**
>
> In a scenario where a knowledge worker, let's call her Anna, is planning and implementing a project, she could benefit from the collective intelligence of her team by seeking the opinions and assessments of her team members. Each team member brings their own experiences, expertise and perspectives to the decision-making process, reducing potential biases and overconfidence that Anna may have.
>
> For example, Anna could use an online platform where team members can share their assessments and suggestions for project planning and implementation. This will involve a broader range of ideas and opinions, leading to the final decision and planning being better based on the collective wisdom of the group, rather than just Anna's individual views.

In this case, System 3's collective intelligence helps reduce Anna's overconfidence in her own abilities and assumptions. She relies more on the wisdom of the group, which leads to more realistic project planning and a higher probability of success.

7.1.3 Availability Heuristic

System 3 can help address the problem of availability heuristics among knowledge workers by providing access to a wider variety of information, experiences and perspectives. By collaborating and sharing knowledge in a group, knowledge workers can overcome their personal biases and make better decisions based on a more comprehensive information base.

> **Example**
>
> Imagine a knowledge worker named Max has to make a decision about introducing a new technology in his company. Max tends to rely on information that is readily available to him, such as the experiences of a colleague friend who has recently introduced a similar technology. This could lead Max to make a decision based on a limited source of information.
>
> However, by drawing on the collective intelligence of his team, other departments or even external experts, Max can gather a wealth of information, experience and perspectives that may not be immediately available. This can be done through regular meetings, brainstorming sessions, online platforms for sharing ideas or access to expert networks.

By incorporating collective intelligence into his decision-making, Max becomes less susceptible to the availability heuristic. The additional information and perspectives enable him to make a better-informed decision about adopting the new technology and reduce the risk of bad decisions due to limited information sources.

7.1.4 Influence of Emotions on Thinking

This section is about System 3 and the influence of emotions on thinking and decision- making. When knowledge workers work together in a team or group, they can bring different perspectives, experiences and ways of thinking. This helps to balance the emotional biases that individual team members may have and contribute to more objective and rational decision-making.

> **Example**
>
> Let's say Julia is a project manager and needs to decide what her team's priorities will be for the next few months. However, she has recently learned that her best friend in another team has been made redundant, which is emotionally stressful for her and may affect her decision-making.
>
> By turning to System 3 and using the collective intelligence of its colleagues and staff, it can benefit from their different opinions and perspectives. The group can collectively make a more objective assessment of priorities by analysing and discussing different aspects of the decision. In this way, the emotional biases that Julia may bring to her decision-making are balanced by the different perspectives and more rational approaches of the other team members.

Overall, System 3 can help reduce the influence of emotions on thinking by basing the decision-making process on the collective intelligence of a group of individuals who bring different perspectives and ways of thinking to the table.

7.1.5 Confirmation Error

Daniel Kahneman describes confirmation bias (also known as confirmation bias) as the human tendency to select, interpret and remember information in a way that confirms one's beliefs or hypotheses. People tend to give more weight to information that supports their views, while giving less weight to conflicting information.

System 3 can help overcome confirmation bias by incorporating different perspectives and experiences into the decision-making process. In an environment where knowledge workers and managers collaborate and share ideas and opinions, they are more likely to consider different views and interpretations rather than just confirming their own beliefs.

> **Example**
> Suppose a team is working on a project and there is disagreement about the best way to proceed. Instead of allowing each individual to remain entrenched in their own beliefs, the team encourages open and constructive discussion where all perspectives are heard and considered. Through this collective collaboration, the team can reduce confirmation bias as different viewpoints and ideas are incorporated into the decision-making process. Tools and methods to promote collective intelligence can also help overcome confirmation bias. For example, brainstorming sessions, structured debates and the involvement of external experts can help to bring different perspectives into the decision-making process and challenge existing beliefs and biases.

Overall, by including different perspectives and encouraging collaboration and open discussion, System 3 can reduce confirmation bias and enable more balanced decision-making.

7.1.6 Framing Effect

The framing effect describes the tendency to make decisions based on the way information is presented or framed rather than on an objective assessment of the underlying facts.

System 3 can mitigate the framing effect in the following aspects:

- **Diverse perspectives:** Collective intelligence incorporates the opinions and perspectives of a wide range of individuals, leading to a more comprehensive and balanced view of a problem or issue. This can help reduce the influence of framing on decision-making.
- **Collaborative decision-making:** In System 3, decisions are made collectively by a group, which can mitigate the individual biases of each member. Collaboration can lead to different framings being discussed and considered, increasing the likelihood of a more objective decision.
- **Reflection and discussion:** Collective intelligence enables participants to share their thoughts, opinions and reflections with each other and to reflect together.
- This open communication can help to identify the framing effect and reduce its influence on decision-making.
- **Sharing experience:** As System 3 is based on the collective experience and knowledge of a group, members can learn from each other and improve their ability to recognise and manage the framing effect.

Overall, System 3 can help reduce the framing effect by including different perspectives, promoting collaboration and reflecting on decisions together.

7.1.7 Anchor Heuristics

An example of the anchor heuristic could occur in a negotiation scenario.

> **Example**
> Imagine a knowledge worker negotiating a salary for a new position. The employer first mentions a salary of 60,000 euros. This amount serves as an anchor and influences the subsequent negotiations. The knowledge worker might now seek a higher salary, but the negotiations might still take place around this anchor value, leading to a possibly suboptimal decision.

System 3, based on collective intelligence, can help cope with the anchor heuristic in several ways:

- **Diversity of opinions:** In a group setting, such as that found in System 3, different perspectives and opinions come together. This diversity can help reduce the impact of an anchor by taking into account different views and experiences.
- **Group discussions:** By sharing information and arguments within a group, members can develop a better understanding of the different aspects of a decision. This enables them to identify and disengage from possible anchors.
- **Expert assessments:** In System 3, experts from different fields can contribute their knowledge and experience. They can help to better assess the importance of an anchor in the context of the decision and show more realistic alternatives.
- **Group decision-making:** Shared decision-making within a group can reduce the influence of individual cognitive biases, such as the anchor heuristic. The group can make a more balanced judgement together and make a better decision.

Overall, System 3 can help reduce the impact of the anchor heuristic through the diversity of opinions, group discussions, expert assessments and group decisions.

7.2 Benefits for the Manager

7.2.1 Management of the New

Peter F. Drucker coined the term "managing the new" to describe the concept whereby managers and organisations constantly seek new opportunities, ideas and changes to achieve their goals and remain competitive. Managing the new is about fostering innovation, managing change, assessing risk and using resources effectively to achieve growth and success.

Managing the new and innovation management are closely related but not identical. Innovation management focuses specifically on the development, implementation and marketing of new ideas, products or services, while managing the new takes a broader perspective. It includes innovation management but also goes beyond it. Managing the new deals with change at different levels, including adapting business models, introducing new technologies, redesigning work processes and responding to changing market conditions.

While innovation management aims at creating new value and sources of growth, managing the new also includes the ability to successfully manage change, assess risks and adapt the whole organisation to new challenges and opportunities. In this sense, managing the new is a broader approach that includes innovation management but also covers other aspects of organisational adaptability and development.

System 3 can be used as a tool for managing the new in different ways:

- **Idea generation:** System 3 can be used to bring together diverse perspectives and ideas from staff, experts and stakeholders to find new approaches and solutions to problems and challenges.
- **Decision-making:** Collective intelligence can help make better decisions by tapping into the collective wisdom and experience of stakeholders. This can lead to the identification and implementation of innovative solutions that contribute to the success of the organisation in both the short and long term.
- **Risk management:** By using System 3, managers can better assess risks by taking into account the opinions and experiences of a wide range of people. This enables a more comprehensive risk assessment and can help to identify potential risks at an early stage and take appropriate countermeasures.
- **Change management:** Collective intelligence can help manage change more effectively by encouraging employee participation and engagement, while drawing on the knowledge and experience of the whole organisation. This can help reduce resistance to change and support the successful implementation of new strategies and initiatives.

> **Example**
> A practical example of the use of System 3 in managing the new is a company that wants to develop a new product idea. To get a wide range of ideas and perspectives, the company could use an online platform where employees, experts and customers can submit and discuss suggestions. By bringing together different opinions and experiences, innovative and promising product ideas can be identified and further developed. Collective intelligence helps to better understand potential risks and challenges and to find suitable solutions.

By using System 3 to promote the management of the new, managers can strengthen the innovative power and adaptability of their organisations and thus ensure sustainable success.

7.2.2 Management of the Existing

Peter Drucker defines managing what exists as the process in which managers and leaders aim to optimise and make efficient the current processes, structures and procedures within an organisation. The main objective is to maintain and improve organisational performance by increasing efficiency, controlling quality, reducing costs and ensuring smooth operations. In contrast to managing the new, managing the existing focuses on the stability and continuity of existing business practices and structures.

System 3, the collective intelligence, can be helpful in managing the existing in various ways:

- **Knowledge sharing and best practices:** By using collective intelligence, companies can better leverage the knowledge and experience of employees and external partners to identify, develop and implement best practices.
- **Problem solving and process optimisation:** Collective intelligence can help identify problems and bottlenecks in existing processes and workflows and develop solutions based on the collective knowledge and experience of those involved.
- **Decision-making:** By accessing a wider range of information and opinions, managers can make more informed decisions in managing

what exists, based on both expert knowledge and the collective experience of staff.
- **Collaboration and teamwork:** The use of collective intelligence promotes collaboration and teamwork within organisations by facilitating knowledge sharing, communication and joint learning.

Overall, System 3 can assist in managing what exists by providing access to the knowledge and experience of a larger group of people, helping to improve organisational performance and efficiency.

7.2.3 Organisation of the Work

Here, first of all, is a summary of the basic tasks for managers that Peter Drucker sees in the context of the organisation of work:

- **Goal setting:** Managers need to define clear goals for their organisation and ensure that all stakeholders understand and work towards these goals.
- **Planning:** Managers need to plan the activities and resources required to achieve the goals.
- **Organisation and structuring:** Managers need to create an effective organisational structure that promotes information flow and collaboration.
- **Delegation and monitoring:** Managers need to delegate tasks and responsibilities to their staff and monitor their progress.
- **Communication:** Managers need to communicate clearly and effectively and ensure an open, transparent working environment.
- **Motivation and development:** Managers need to motivate, develop and encourage their staff to increase their performance and commitment.

System 3 can help managers with these tasks in several ways:

- In goal setting, System 3 can help to achieve a broader understanding and acceptance of the goals through the exchange of ideas and experiences within the organisation or with external experts.

- In the planning phase, System 3 can be used to gather information, insights and opinions from various sources that can enrich and improve the planning process.
- System 3 can help with organisation and structure, through platforms and tools that promote collaboration, knowledge sharing and information flow.
- In delegation and monitoring, System 3 can help managers better track the progress of projects and tasks by providing information and feedback from staff and teams.
- In communication, System 3 can promote collaboration and the exchange of information across departmental and hierarchical boundaries, resulting in a more open and transparent working environment.
- In staff motivation and development, System 3 can help support staff's professional development and enhance their skills by providing access to knowledge, expertise and resources from across the network.

Overall, System 3 can help managers make their organisation more effective and promote collaboration, communication and development within the company.

7.2.4 Benefits in the Context of the Principles

A tool based on collective intelligence can support several of the management principles established by Peter Drucker:

- **Management by objectives (MBO):** System 3 can help identify goals within an organisation by using the collective wisdom of employees. This can be done by using surveys, polls or brainstorming platforms to collectively develop and evaluate goals and priorities.
- **Time management:** By drawing on the collective experience and best practices within the organisation, System 3 can help identify and implement time management strategies that improve productivity.
- **Effective decision-making:** System 3 enables managers to gather different perspectives and opinions from staff and thus make more

informed decisions. Collective intelligence can help uncover possible biases and blind spots and increase the quality of decisions.
- **Communication and collaboration:** System 3 can provide communication and collaboration platforms that promote the exchange of information and ideas and enable knowledge and skills to be used effectively within the organisation.
- **Innovation and continuous improvement:** By crowdsourcing employees' ideas and suggestions, System 3 can help identify and drive innovation and improvement within the organisation. Crowdsourcing initiatives or idea management systems can help identify and implement creative solutions and improvements.

These examples show how System 3 can foster collective intelligence and collaboration within an organisation to support effective management and better decision-making.

7.3 Benefits for the Company

> Reducing the intelligence of the enterprise, that is the available knowledge and cognitive potential, to that of a single person, is a form of "parochialism" that is unnecessary. (Simon, 2004)

By drawing on collective intelligence, the company can identify innovative approaches that it might otherwise have overlooked. At the same time, it promotes collaboration and the sharing of knowledge and experience among stakeholders, leading to a better understanding of customer needs and a more effective use of resources.

> **Example**
> One example is crowdsourcing of ideas and feedback: A company could create an internal or external platform where employees, partners and customers can submit, discuss and evaluate ideas. This gives the company valuable insights into the needs and desires of customers and allows it to target its resources to develop solutions that meet those needs.

In this way, System 3 can help the company deliver value to the customer with the resources it uses by harnessing the collective wisdom and knowledge of employees, partners and even customers to develop better products, services and solutions.

> **Summary**
>
> This chapter has explored the benefits of System 3 for knowledge workers, managers and companies. Collective intelligence can help mitigate cognitive biases and improve decision-making processes. Integrating System 3 into everyday work can help knowledge workers benefit from the wisdom of crowds and incorporate different perspectives into their work.
> For the management of the new, System 3 can serve as a tool for generating innovative ideas and solutions, while in the management of the existing it helps to optimise processes and resources. Furthermore, collective intelligence supports the organisation of work and task completion according to Drucker's principles. Finally, System 3 can help companies better identify customer needs and target resources to develop customer-oriented solutions.

References

Drucker, P. F. (1974). *New management practice. Volume 1 - Tasks Volume 2 - Methods*. Econ-Verlag.

Franken, R., & Franken, S. (2011). *Integriertes Wissens- und Innovationsmanagement. With case studies and examples from corporate practice*. Gabler.

Kahneman, D. (2012). *Fast thinking, slow thinking*. Siedler Verlag.

Lévy, P. (1997). *Collective intelligence. Mankind's emerging world in cyberspace*. Plenum Trade.

Simon, F. B. (2004). *Together we are stupid!? The intelligence of companies, managers and markets*. Carl-Auer-Systeme-Verl.

Surowiecki, J. (2007). *The wisdom of the many. Warum Gruppen klüger sind als Einzelne // [Why groups are smarter than individuals]*. Goldmann.

8

Concrete Application of System 3: The Collective Intelligence

8.1 Requirements and Prerequisites

8.1.1 Technological Requirements

The successful implementation and use of System 3, a computer-based decision support system (DSS) that uses collective intelligence, depends on a number of technological requirements. In this section, we will explain the key technological requirements that organisations should consider in order to effectively deploy System 3 and reap the benefits of this technology. We will also consider exemplary collective intelligence tools and platforms.

- **Data infrastructure and data management:** A powerful System 3 requires a solid data infrastructure and effective data management. This includes the collection, storage, processing and analysis of data from various sources inside and outside the organisation. To use collective intelligence effectively, companies should be able to process a variety of data, including texts, surveys, opinions, ideas and feedback from employees, customers and other stakeholders.

> **Example**
> An example of this is a company that implements an internal idea management system to collect suggestions and feedback from employees. The company can then use this data to drive innovation, optimise work processes and increase employee satisfaction.

By implementing an effective data management system, the company can ensure that valuable information is efficiently collected, analysed and integrated into decision-making processes to take full advantage of collective intelligence.

- **Platforms and tools for collective intelligence:** The adoption of tools and platforms that promote collective intelligence is critical to the success of System 3. Solutions such as those offered by CrowdWorX[1] and Innosabi[2] enable companies to collect, analyse and use the knowledge, experience and expertise of a large number of individuals. These platforms offer functions such as idea management, collaboration, discussion, evaluation and decision-making, thus facilitating the effective use of collective intelligence in the decision-making process.
- **Integration with existing systems:** The successful implementation of System 3 requires integration with the company's existing information systems and business processes. This includes connecting to databases, ERP and CRM systems and providing interfaces for data exchange between the different systems. Seamless integration enables companies to fully exploit the potential of collective intelligence while maintaining the efficiency and effectiveness of their existing processes.
- **Security and data protection:** Security and protection of data are critical factors for the successful deployment of System 3. Organisations must ensure that their collective intelligence systems and platforms comply with applicable data protection regulations and are protected

---

[1] https://www.crowdworx.com/de/
[2] https://innosabi.com/

from unauthorised access, loss or tampering. This can be achieved through appropriate security measures such as encryption, authentication, access control and regular security audits.

8.1.2 Organisational Requirements

In addition to the technological requirements, organisational aspects also play a crucial role in the successful use of System 3. Companies need to adapt their internal structures, processes and cultures to effectively use collective intelligence and benefit from the advantages of this technology. This section discusses the key organisational requirements for the application of System 3 at the company level.

- **Culture of cooperation and openness:** A corporate culture that promotes collaboration, openness and the sharing of knowledge and ideas is crucial for the successful use of System 3. Employees should be encouraged to actively participate in discussions, contribute their opinions and perspectives and provide constructive feedback. Such a culture creates an environment where collective intelligence can flourish and be used effectively in decision-making processes.
- **Clear processes and responsibilities:** To use System 3 effectively, companies need to define clear processes and responsibilities for using collective intelligence in their decision-making processes. This includes identifying relevant stakeholders, defining communication channels and establishing mechanisms for idea evaluation, prioritisation and decision-making. Through transparent and structured processes, companies can ensure that collective intelligence is effectively integrated into their decision-making processes.
- **Competence development and training:** To realise the full potential of System 3, companies need to invest in skills development and training for their employees. This includes teaching the skills and knowledge needed to effectively use collective intelligence, such as

collaboration, communication, critical thinking and problem-solving. Through continuous training and development, companies can ensure that their employees are able to use System 3 effectively and contribute to the company's success.
- **Leadership support:** The active support and commitment of leaders is critical to the successful use of System 3. Leaders need to recognise and promote the importance of collective intelligence and create a culture that supports the use of System 3. They should serve as role models and encourage their staff to participate in collective decision-making and openly share their ideas and opinions.
- **Evaluation and continuous improvement:** Finally, companies should regularly evaluate the use of System 3 and the results of collective decision-making. By monitoring performance indicators and analysing success stories and challenges, companies can gain valuable insights and continuously improve their strategies and processes related to System 3. Systematic evaluation enables companies to learn from their experiences, identify best practices and further optimise their use of collective intelligence.

The organisational requirements for applying System 3 at the corporate level include creating a culture of collaboration and openness, establishing clear processes and responsibilities, investing in skills development and training, leadership support and continuous evaluation and improvement. By addressing these aspects, companies can effectively reap the benefits of collective intelligence and maximise the power of System 3.

8.1.3 Employee Competencies

Employee competencies for the application of System 3 (collective intelligence) include a range of skills and abilities required for the effective use of collective intelligence within an organisation. These include:

- **Communication and collaboration:** To use collective intelligence effectively, staff must be able to share information and ideas openly and constructively. Good communication skills and a willingness to

8 Concrete Application of System 3: The Collective Intelligence

work together in teams are essential for the successful application of System 3.

- **Critical thinking and problem-solving:** Employees using collective intelligence must be able to critically evaluate information and ideas from different sources and draw conclusions. They should also be creative and have problem-solving skills to develop innovative solutions to complex challenges.
- **Adaptability and willingness to learn:** The use of collective intelligence often requires a change in the way employees work and think. Therefore, adaptability and willingness to learn new skills and adapt to changing working conditions are crucial.
- **Self-management and initiative:** Employees using collective intelligence must be able to manage their time and resources effectively, set priorities and work independently. Self-initiative and a sense of responsibility are also important to contribute and implement ideas and suggestions.
- **Openness and empathy:** To use collective intelligence successfully, employees need to be open to new ideas, perspectives and approaches. Empathy and the ability to understand the needs and perspectives of others are also important to create an inclusive and productive work environment that fosters collective intelligence.

By developing these competencies in employees, organisations can maximise the benefits of collective intelligence and create a culture of collaboration, innovation and continuous improvement.

8.2 Implementation

In the section "Implementing System 3" we will focus on the practical application of collective intelligence in organisations. The successful implementation of System 3 requires careful planning, implementation and integration into existing work processes. In this section we will explain the different steps and aspects to be considered when implementing System 3.

First we will look at planning and design, which is about defining the goals and requirements of the project, choosing the right tools and methods and developing a project plan. In this part we will also refer to the sections on employee competences and corporate culture in order to create an environment that supports and encourages collective intelligence.

In the next subchapter we will focus on the implementation of the first project. Here we will discuss the practical aspects of implementing System 3, including identifying the right project teams, working with internal and external stakeholders and continuously monitoring and adjusting the project to ensure success.

Finally, we will look at integrating System 3 into existing processes. In this part, we will discuss the challenges and opportunities in introducing collective intelligence into everyday work, including adapting workflows, ensuring data quality and data protection and continuously improving and scaling System 3 applications.

By successfully implementing System 3, organisations can benefit from collective intelligence to develop innovative solutions to complex challenges, increase efficiency and foster a culture of collaboration and continuous learning.

8.2.1 Planning and Conception

In this section we will look at the planning and design of System 3, collective intelligence. The implementation of System 3 requires careful planning to ensure that the organisation can reap the benefits of collective intelligence. Here are the key steps and considerations in planning and designing System 3 projects:

- **Define goals and requirements:** Start by identifying the goals you want to achieve by implementing System 3. These may include, for example, improving decision-making, increasing innovation or improving collaboration. Make sure that the goals and requirements are clearly defined and measurable in order to assess the success of the project.

8 Concrete Application of System 3: The Collective Intelligence

- **Selecting the right technologies and methods:** Investigate the available technologies and methods for collective intelligence to select those that best fit your goals and requirements. These include platforms and tools that allow knowledge and ideas to be collected, organised and analysed from a variety of sources, such as those from CrowdWorX or Innosabi.
- **Foster a supportive corporate culture:** Successful implementation of System 3 requires a culture that encourages collaboration, openness and the sharing of knowledge and ideas. Ensure that managers and employees understand the importance of collective intelligence and are willing to share their knowledge and expertise.
- **Create a project plan:** Develop a detailed project plan that maps out the different phases of the project, the resources required and the responsibilities of team members. A good project plan will enable you to monitor the progress of the project, identify risks and take action to mitigate them.

The following specific steps should be included in the project plan:

1. **Needs analysis:** Identify the specific needs and challenges of your organisation where the collective intelligence of employees and customers can add value. This could include identifying new product ideas, improving existing processes or solving complex problems.
2. **Selecting tools:** Investigate the tools available to tap into collective intelligence and select those that best fit your organisation's needs and requirements. These may include idea management platforms, crowdsourcing or social networks.
3. **Integration into existing systems: Ensure** that the selected tools can be easily integrated into your organisation's existing systems and processes. This may involve adapting the tools to existing IT infrastructures or creating interfaces to other internal systems.
4. **Training and onboarding:** Plan training and onboarding programmes for staff and clients to provide them with the necessary knowledge and skills to use the selected tools effectively. This can include training, workshops or webinars.

5. **Communication and marketing:** Develop a communication and marketing strategy to promote the adoption of the tools within the organisation and with clients. This may include internal communication campaigns, incentive programmes or targeted marketing campaigns.
6. **Carry out a pilot project:** This is addressed in the section "Implement the First Project" goes into detail.
7. **Evaluation and adaptation:** This is the subject of the section "Evaluation and Optimisation" goes into detail.
8. **Organisation-wide introduction:** After successful completion of the pilot project and adjustments, introduce the tools organisation-wide and integrate them into the daily work of employees and customers.

- **Identify and develop staff competencies: Ensure** that your staff have the necessary competencies to use System 3 effectively. These include technical expertise, collaborative skills and critical thinking and problem-solving skills. Invest in staff training and encourage knowledge sharing and learning within the organisation.

8.2.2 Implement the First Project

In the following, an example project is presented that illustrates the implementation of collective intelligence in a company. Based on this example, the steps of the project implementation are described to give an insight into the practical application of System 3.

> **Example**
>
> A medium-sized company wants to use the collective intelligence of its employees to generate innovative ideas for improving its product range. The company decides to use a crowdsourcing platform to collect and evaluate ideas and feedback from employees.
>
> - **Project definition:** The company first defines the goal of the project—in this case the generation of innovative product ideas—and determines the scope, resources and time frame.

- **Platform selection:** The responsible persons evaluate different crowdsourcing platforms that meet the requirements of the project and decide on the most suitable solution.
- **Training and preparation:** Before the launch of the platform, staff and managers are trained in the use of the platform and informed about the project. This ensures that everyone involved has the necessary skills and knowledge to use the platform effectively.
- **Project launch and communication:** The company officially launches the project and communicates the start and objectives of the project to all employees. Clear and transparent communication is crucial to encourage employee participation and ensure that all stakeholders understand the goals and expectations of the project.
- **Idea collection and evaluation:** Employees use the crowdsourcing platform to submit their ideas and suggestions. The platform allows staff to evaluate ideas and provide feedback. This process of collecting and evaluating ideas is iterative and continuous to ensure that the best ideas are identified and developed.
- **Selection and implementation of ideas:** After completing the collection and evaluation of ideas, the company selects the best ideas and develops a plan to implement them. This plan should include the necessary resources, responsibilities and timeframes for implementing the ideas.
- **Evaluation and continuous improvement:** After the implementation of the selected ideas, the company evaluates the results and the success of the project. The insights gained are used to optimise and continuously improve future collective intelligence projects.

By implementing this example project, the company can effectively use the collective intelligence of its employees to generate innovative ideas and improve its product range. This example further illustrates the different steps involved in implementing a project to tap into collective intelligence and shows how companies can successfully integrate System 3 into their workflows.

The experience gained from this first project will help the company to initiate and implement further projects on the use of collective intelligence in the future. In doing so, the company can build on the lessons learned and best practices from the first project and continuously improve the effectiveness of its collective intelligence approaches.

8.2.3 Integration into Existing Processes

For the crowdsourcing project we used as an example in the context of System 3, integration into existing processes means the following steps:

- **Process analysis and optimisation:** Analyse your current processes for idea collection, feedback and collaboration. Identify areas where crowdsourcing platforms or tools can provide an effective solution, such as innovation management, process improvement or strategic decision-making. Optimise these processes by integrating crowdsourcing solutions where they will bring the most benefit.
- **Interfaces and system integration: Ensure** that the crowdsourcing platform or tool is seamlessly integrated into the existing IT infrastructure, such as intranet, project management systems and communication platforms. This enables the smooth exchange of ideas, feedback and results between employees and departments.
- **Change management:** Communicate openly with your employees about the introduction of crowdsourcing and the benefits it will bring to the company and employees. Provide training and support for employees to ease the transition and address any concerns.
- **Roles and responsibilities:** Clarify the responsibilities for monitoring, moderating and evaluating the ideas and feedback collected on the crowdsourcing platform or tool. Clearly define the roles of staff responsible for implementing ideas, collaborating and further developing the system.
- **Performance measurement and monitoring:** Develop KPIs and metrics to monitor the success of the crowdsourcing initiative. Measure

employee participation, quality of ideas submitted, implementation of improvements and impact on the business. Use this data to continuously improve the crowdsourcing initiative and adapt it to changing conditions.
- **Long-term strategy and evolution:** Consider crowdsourcing integration as part of a long-term strategy to foster innovation and collaboration in your organisation. Plan for the continuous development of the crowdsourcing platform or tool and adapt it to new technologies, business needs and employee needs.

8.3 Evaluation and Optimisation

8.3.1 Evaluate Results

The evaluation of the results of the pilot project on collective intelligence is a crucial step to assess the success of the project and to gain important insights for future initiatives. The following aspects should be considered when analysing the results:

- **Quantitative evaluation:** Determine the number of ideas, suggestions and feedback generated, as well as the number of staff and customers involved. This data will help you measure the level of participation and engagement.
- **Qualitative evaluation:** Evaluate the quality of the ideas and proposals submitted in terms of their originality, feasibility and relevance for the company. This will give you an impression of the innovative power of the collective intelligence.
- **Identify trends and patterns:** Examine the results to identify common themes, concerns or areas of focus. This will help you to identify possible areas for improvement or opportunities for the company.
- **Measuring success:** Compare the results achieved with the goals and success criteria set at the beginning of the project. This will allow you to evaluate the success of the project and make adjustments for future projects if necessary.

- **Feedback from participants:** Collect feedback from the participants of the project to capture their experiences, opinions and suggestions for improvement. This will help you to evaluate the project from the perspective of the participants and to further optimise the processes in future projects.

8.3.2 Use of the Knowledge Gained

The insights gained in the pilot project can be used in a variety of ways to improve the performance and efficiency of the company and to increase innovation. Here are some starting points on how you can use the lessons learned:

- **Informed decision-making:** The ideas, suggestions and feedback collected provide a solid basis for informed decision-making. Use this information to make strategic decisions, product developments or process improvements in the company.
- **Identification of potential for improvement:** The analysis of the results enables you to identify areas where there is potential for improvement or innovation. Use these findings to initiate targeted measures to increase your company's performance and competitiveness.
- **Encourage employee engagement:** Involving employees and customers in the collective intelligence pilot shows them that their opinions and ideas are valued. Use the insights gained to increase employee engagement and satisfaction and foster a culture of collaboration and innovation within the company.
- **Adjust strategy:** The insights gained can help to adjust and realign the business strategy by identifying new opportunities, challenges and trends. Adjust your strategy accordingly to keep your business viable and competitive.

8.3.3 Continuous Improvement

One of the essential components to ensure the success of System 3 implementation in the long term is continuous improvement. This means that companies should constantly work to develop their processes, tools and use of collective intelligence to increase the efficiency and effectiveness of their decision-making and innovation.

Continuous improvement can take place in different areas, such as

- **Process improvement:** Regularly review the processes you use to collect, analyse and implement ideas and feedback within System 3. Identify possible bottlenecks or inefficiencies and take action to address them.
- **Tool optimisation:** Continuously evaluate the tools and technologies used to ensure that they are effective and user-friendly. Be open to implementing new technologies that can further improve the collective intelligence process.
- **Staff development:** Invest in training and development for your staff to ensure they have the skills and knowledge to participate effectively in System 3 and implement the lessons learned.
- **Feedback loops:** Implement feedback loops to continuously receive feedback from staff, customers and other stakeholders. Use this feedback to further optimise your approaches by using collective intelligence.
- **Performance measurement: Use** metrics and indicators to measure and continuously improve the success of your collective intelligence initiatives. Use these metrics to track progress and uncover potential areas for improvement.

8.4 Further Application Examples

Here are some more application examples for the use of System 3 (collective intelligence):

- **Product development:** Use the collective intelligence of employees, customers and partners to collect and evaluate ideas for new products or improvements to existing products.
- **Marketing and sales:** Collect customer feedback and opinions on marketing campaigns, sales strategies or market positioning to optimise your marketing and sales activities.

- **Human resource management:** Capture employees' opinions and suggestions on topics such as work environment, company culture and career development to improve employee satisfaction and retention.
- **Knowledge management:** Create a central platform where employees can share their expertise, experiences and best practices to promote knowledge management in the company.
- **Innovation management:** Promote company-wide innovation initiatives by encouraging employees to contribute ideas for process improvements, technology innovations or new business models.
- **Decision-making:** Gather opinions, perspectives and information from a variety of sources to make informed decisions based on a broad knowledge base and a variety of opinions.
- **Customer relationship management:** Use the collective intelligence of customers to identify problems and develop solutions that increase customer satisfaction and loyalty.
- **Crisis management:** Collect real-time information and assessments from employees, customers and partners to react quickly to crisis situations and take effective action.

These examples show that System 3 can be used in a wide range of sectors and industries to harness the collective intelligence of employees, customers and partners for better decisions, innovation and business success.

Checklist for the Implementation

1. Define the objective:
Identify the specific goals and outcomes you want to achieve by using System 3.

2. Check technological requirements:
Evaluate the existing IT infrastructure and identify which tools and technologies are needed to support System 3.

3. Check organisational requirements:
Check whether your organisation is ready to integrate collective intelligence into existing processes and structures.

4. **Develop employee competencies:**
   Develop the necessary skills and knowledge of your staff to use System 3 effectively.
5. **Planning and conception:**
   Develop a detailed project plan covering all aspects of System 3 implementation.
6. **Implement first project:**
   Select a pilot project to test the use of System 3 and gain experience.
7. **Integration into existing processes:**
   Integrate System 3 into your existing workflows and processes step by step to ensure a smooth implementation.
8. **Evaluate and use results:**
   Monitor the results of System 3 deployment, draw conclusions and adjust your strategies accordingly.
9. **Scaling and expansion:**
   After you have successfully implemented a pilot project, scale the use of System 3 to other areas and projects in your company.
10. **Continuous improvement:**
    Regularly review the use of System 3 and look for ways to increase its effectiveness and efficiency.

References

Drucker, P. F. (2002). *What is management. The best from 50 years.* ECON.

Lévy, P. (1997). *Collective intelligence. Mankind's emerging world in cyberspace.* Plenum Trade.

Part III

Artificial Intelligence as a System 4

It's not about replacing human intelligence with artificial intelligence. It's about supplementing human intelligence with artificial intelligence.—Ginni Rometty, former CEO of IBM [Wall17]

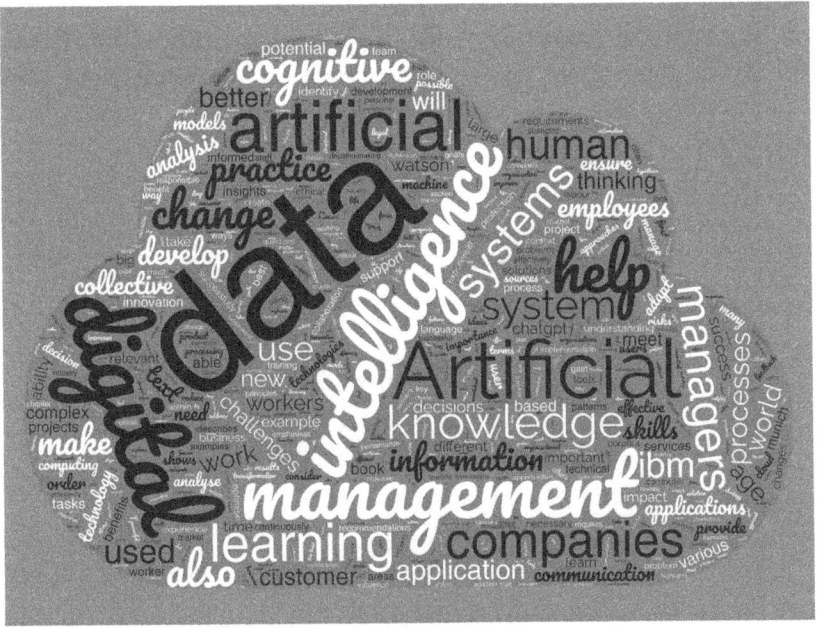

84 Artificial Intelligence as a System 4

1.1 Outlook for Part III

In Part III of this book, we will explore another crucial tool that can help to successfully meet the increased demands and challenges in a digital and ever-changing world: artificial intelligence, which we refer to as System 4 (see Fig. 1).

At the beginning of Chap. 9 we will introduce System 4 and define artificial intelligence. We will explain the various technologies and approaches that are subsumed under this term and discuss the differences and similarities to other forms of intelligence, especially collective intelligence. We will then look at application fields of artificial intelligence and present successful implementations in different industries and contexts.

In Chap. 10 we will focus on the benefits of System 4 for knowledge workers, managers and companies. We will analyse how artificial intelligence can contribute to addressing the requirements identified in Part 1 and what the benefits are for the different stakeholders.

Chapter 11 is dedicated to the practical application of System 4. We will highlight the requirements for implementing artificial intelligence systems and provide step-by-step instructions on how to carry out a first

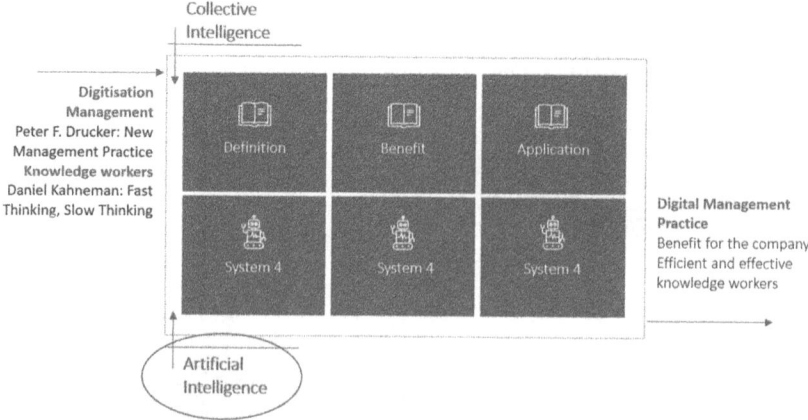

Fig. 1 Definition, benefits and application of collective intelligence as a System 4

AI project. In addition, we will explore the evaluation and use of artificial intelligence results and present further examples of successful applications. Finally, we will present best practices and success factors for implementing System 4 in your own context and provide a checklist to facilitate the process.

By the end of Part III, you will have gained a sound understanding of AI as a tool to address the challenges of digital transformation. With this knowledge, you will be able to make informed decisions about the use of System 4 in your organisation and pave the way for a successful integration of artificial intelligence.

9

Presentation of System 4: The Concept of Artificial Intelligence

9.1 Definition

As Ginni Rometty, the former CEO of IBM, aptly observed, "It's not about replacing human intelligence with artificial intelligence. It's about supplementing human intelligence with artificial intelligence." With this in mind, we will explore how AI, referred to as System 4, can help augment human capabilities, optimise workflows and help organisations better meet the challenges of digitalisation. Our focus is on the synergy of human and artificial intelligence and how this collaboration can improve the effectiveness and efficiency of knowledge workers, managers and organisations as a whole.

There are various definitions of artificial intelligence (AI), which vary depending on the perspective and focus of application. Here are some common definitions:

1. **AI as a simulation of human intelligence:** Artificial intelligence is a branch of computer science that deals with simulating human intelligence processes, such as learning, perception, problem solving and decision making, by computers and machines.

2. **AI as machine learning:** Artificial intelligence refers to algorithms and methods that enable computers to learn from data and improve their performance on a given task without having to be explicitly programmed.
3. **AI as expert systems:** Artificial intelligence refers to computer systems that replicate human expert knowledge in a specific area and are able to solve problems that would normally require human experts.
4. **AI as autonomous agents:** Artificial intelligence comprises intelligent agents or systems that are able to make autonomous decisions and act in their environment to achieve specific goals.

In the context of your book, which focuses on knowledge work, management and digitalisation, the first definition fits best:

AI as a simulation of human intelligence: Artificial intelligence is a branch of computer science that deals with simulating human intelligence processes, such as learning, perception, problem solving and decision making, by computers and machines.

This definition emphasises the aspect of complementing human intelligence and capabilities, which is particularly relevant in the context of your book. It emphasises the role of AI in improving the efficiency and effectiveness of knowledge workers, managers and companies as a whole.

The development of artificial intelligence (AI) has gone through various phases over the years and encompasses several subfields. Here is a brief overview of the phases and subfields of AI:

1. **Early beginnings (1943–1955):** In this phase, the theoretical foundations of AI were laid by the work of Warren McCulloch and Walter Pitts on artificial neurons and their networks. Alan Turing developed the Turing Test as a measure of machine intelligence during this period.
2. **Classical AI (1956–1974):** This phase began with the Dartmouth Conference in 1956, at which AI was established as an independent field of research. The first AI programmes based on symbolic processing and logical reasoning emerged during this period. There were advances in chess, machine translation and natural language processing.

9 Presentation of System 4: The Concept of Artificial Intelligence

3. **AI Winter (1974–1980):** This phase saw a disillusionment with the initial expectations of AI. The lack of progress and the high costs led to a reduction in funding and the so-called AI winter.
4. **Neural networks and expert systems (1980–1987):** In this phase, AI experienced a renaissance through the rediscovery of neural networks, especially the backpropagation algorithm. At the same time, expert systems were developed based on knowledge bases and inference mechanisms.
5. **Machine learning and data mining (1988–2010):** In this phase, machine learning, especially statistical machine learning, moved into the focus of AI research. Data mining, the discovery of patterns in large amounts of data, also became an important subfield of AI.
6. **Deep learning and AI revolution (2011–present):** The introduction of deep learning, a class of neural networks with many layers, led to an AI revolution and impressive advances in image recognition, speech recognition, machine translation, game strategies and autonomous driving.

An example from the first phase of artificial intelligence is the programme "Logic Theorist", which was developed by Allen Newell and Herbert A. Simon in 1956. Logic Theorist was one of the first AI programs and was developed to create mathematical proofs. It was based on symbolic processing and logical reasoning. The programme was able to find proofs for mathematical problems by automatically drawing conclusions from axioms and statements that had already been proven.

One example from the current phase of AI is DeepMind's neural network "AlphaGo", which won the Go World Championship in 2016 against the human Go master Lee Sedol. Go is an ancient Chinese board game that was considered particularly challenging for artificial intelligence due to its complexity and the enormous number of possible moves. AlphaGo's victory was seen as a crucial breakthrough in AI research because the system was able to show human-like intuition and creative thinking to beat a world-class player in a game previously considered unattainable for machines.

This event led to a broad public discussion about the potential of AI and the possible impact on different areas of life and work, including the role of AI in knowledge work and digitalisation.

The examples illustrate the enormous development in AI research, from symbolic processing and logical reasoning in the early phase to deep learning and reinforcement learning in the current phase. These advances have made it possible for AI to be used in various subfields, such as:

- **Machine learning (ML):** A subfield of AI that develops algorithms and methods to enable computers to learn from data.
- **Deep learning:** A subset of ML that focuses on artificial neural networks with many layers.
- **Expert systems:** AI systems that replicate human expert knowledge in a specific area and solve problems that would normally require human experts.
- **Natural language processing (NLP):** A subfield of AI that deals with the interaction between computers and human language.

9.2 Delimitation

In the context of this book, which focuses on knowledge work and digitalisation, the subfields of machine learning, deep learning, natural language processing, computer vision and knowledge-based systems are of particular interest, as they are directly applicable to many aspects of knowledge work and digital transformation and offer significant added value.

1. **Machine learning (ML) and deep learning:** These subfields make it possible to efficiently analyse large amounts of data and to recognise patterns that would be difficult for humans to detect. In knowledge work, recognising patterns and correlations in data is crucial to making informed decisions, optimising processes and developing innovative solutions. With the help of ML and deep learning techniques, knowledge workers can extract and use information from data faster and more accurately.

9 Presentation of System 4: The Concept of Artificial Intelligence

2. **Natural Language Processing (NLP):** NLP enables computers to understand, interpret and generate human language. Communication plays a central role in knowledge work, and NLP techniques can help facilitate communication and information exchange between knowledge workers, managers and systems. NLP can also be used to analyse large amounts of textual data, create summaries, identify key concepts and even generate human-like text.
3. **Computer Vision:** The ability of computers to recognise and interpret images and videos is relevant to many aspects of knowledge work and digitalisation. Computer vision makes it possible to develop automated inspection systems, improve surveillance and security systems and create interactive user experiences in applications and web services. In knowledge work, computer vision can help to use and process visual information more efficiently.
4. **Knowledge-based systems:** These systems use knowledge and experience to solve problems and make decisions. In knowledge work, it is crucial to be able to draw on existing knowledge and generate new knowledge. Knowledge-based systems can include expert systems, decision support systems or intelligent agents that help knowledge workers and managers make informed decisions and solve complex problems more efficiently.

Overall, these subfields of artificial intelligence offer technologies and tools that can support and optimise knowledge work and digitisation in many ways by enhancing human capabilities, automating processes and enabling innovative solutions.

9.3 Fields of Application

Artificial intelligence is used today in a wide range of practical application fields. Here is an overview of some of the most important applications:

1. **Medicine and healthcare:** AI is used to diagnose diseases, analyse medical images, predict disease progression and personalise treatment plans.
2. **Financial services:** AI helps with fraud identification, risk management, lending, portfolio management and algorithm-based trading.

3. **Logistics and transport:** AI supports the optimisation of supply chains, traffic flow control, route planning, autonomous vehicles and drones.
4. **Marketing and sales:** AI enables personalised customer targeting, recommendation systems, customer engagement and segmentation and automated chatbots for customer support.
5. **Manufacturing and production:** AI contributes to the automation of production processes, quality control, predictive maintenance and product development.
6. **Energy and environment:** AI assists in optimising energy consumption, monitoring and forecasting environmental impacts, climate modelling and renewable energy.
7. **Education and research:** AI is used in adaptive learning systems, automated assessment, curriculum development and research support.

In this book, we focus on the application of Artificial Intelligence in the context of the knowledge worker facing the challenges of digitalisation. Knowledge workers are often faced with complex problems that require quick decisions and innovative solutions. AI technologies can help knowledge workers analyse data more efficiently, gain new insights, improve communication and create collaborative work environments.

In this context, machine learning, deep learning, natural language processing and knowledge-based systems can help to enhance the skills of knowledge workers and enable them to work more effectively and efficiently. As a result, they are better equipped to successfully meet the growing demands and challenges of digitalisation and to develop innovative solutions in their respective fields.

Summary

In this chapter we have presented the development of artificial intelligence (AI) and its different phases and subfields. Particularly relevant to the context of the book are the subfields of machine learning, deep learning, natural language processing, computer vision and knowledge-based systems. We have also provided an overview of practical application fields of AI and highlighted its role in addressing the challenges of digitalisation and knowledge work.

9 Presentation of System 4: The Concept of Artificial Intelligence

> Now that we have examined the various aspects and fields of application of artificial intelligence, especially in the context of digitalisation and knowledge work, in the next chapter we will focus on how System 4—artificial intelligence—can concretely contribute to providing significant added value to knowledge workers, managers and companies. We will analyse the benefits and potentials of System 4 in detail, showing how it can help to effectively manage the challenges of the modern world of work and increase the performance of all stakeholders.

Reference

Paz, B. J. (2020). Kai-Fu-Lee (2019): AI Superpowers-China, Silicon Valley and the New World Order. *AI & Society, 3*(35), 771–772.

Online Sources

Wall Street Journal: IBM CEO: AI Will Be Man and Machine, Not Man vs. Machine. https://www.wsj.com/video/ibm-ceo-ai-will-be-man-and-machine-not-man-vs-machine/74769095-C3C1-4173-9269-AAE812B0D340.html?mod=Searchresults_pos11&page=1, as of 27/03/2023

10

Benefits of System 4: Artificial Intelligence

10.1 Benefits for the Knowledge Worker

10.1.1 Distortions in Perception

Artificial intelligence (AI) can help deal with biases in the perception of probabilities and risks by being based on objective data and algorithms that are independent of human biases. Here are some ways System 4 can help:

- **Data analytics:** AI systems can process and analyse large amounts of data quickly and efficiently to identify patterns, correlations and probabilities. This can help produce objective and data-based assessments of risks and probabilities that are less susceptible to human bias.
- **Predictive models:** Artificial intelligence can be used to develop predictive models based on historical data that forecast future events and probabilities. These models can help reduce human bias in the perception of probabilities and risks by providing objective and informed forecasts.

- **Decision support:** AI-based systems can serve as decision support by providing recommendations and assessments based on data and algorithms. This allows knowledge workers to make informed decisions that are less influenced by personal biases.
- **Bias detection:** Artificial intelligence can be used to detect and point out human biases in decision-making processes. This can help knowledge workers become aware of their own cognitive biases and actively take them into account in their decision-making processes.
- **Personalised interventions:** AI systems can be used to develop personalised interventions and training based on the individual biases and needs of knowledge workers. These interventions can help improve perceptions of probabilities and risks and reduce biases.

> **Example**
>
> Suppose a knowledge worker is part of a project team in a company that is involved in developing new products. The team has to decide which product ideas to invest in, based on expected success and risks.
>
> Without AI support, the team might be susceptible to biases in their perception of probabilities and risks. For example, due to availability heuristics, they might tend to favour product ideas based on similar, recently successful products rather than considering all relevant information and data.
>
> This is where System 4 comes in: the AI system can analyse large amounts of data from various sources such as market analyses, sales figures, customer feedback and competitive analysis to create objective assessments of the potential for success and the risks of the various product ideas.
>
> The AI system can also develop predictive models to simulate the expected success of product ideas under different scenarios and market conditions. These models can help the team make an informed decision about the best investment opportunities that is less influenced by human bias.
>
> In addition, AI can provide decision support by presenting recommendations based on the analysed data and forecasts. These recommendations can help the team to systematically and objectively evaluate the different product ideas and select those that offer the greatest potential for success and profitability.
>
> Finally, the AI system can also be used to raise the team's awareness of possible biases in their decisions by highlighting which factors might influence their perception of probabilities and risks.

Overall, System 4, artificial intelligence, can help mitigate biases in perceptions of probabilities and risks by providing objective, data-based information and analysis to support decision-making. This can lead to knowledge workers making better-informed and less biased decisions.

10.1.2 Overconfidence

Artificial intelligence (System 4) can help reduce overconfidence among knowledge workers by providing objective data, analysis and feedback to help assess actual skills and knowledge more realistically. Here are some ways AI can be used in this context:

- **Performance analysis:** AI can be used to objectively analyse and evaluate a knowledge worker's performance in specific tasks or projects. By providing this information, AI can help the knowledge worker develop a more accurate understanding of their actual skills and limitations, which can lead to a more realistic self-assessment.
- **Feedback and recommendations:** AI systems can provide personalised feedback and recommendations for improvement based on analysis of performance data, work patterns and skills. This can help knowledge workers better understand their strengths and weaknesses and make targeted efforts to improve their skills.
- **Decision support:** AI can also act as a decision support system, assisting the knowledge worker in choosing courses of action. By providing objective data, forecasts and scenario analysis, AI can help the knowledge worker make more informed decisions, relying less on intuition or overconfidence.
- **Team-based decision-making:** AI can also be used to support collaboration and decision-making in teams. By taking into account different perspectives and opinions, AI can help balance individual overconfidence among team members and contribute to more inclusive and balanced decision-making.

Here is a practical example in a project management scenario.

> **Example**
>
> Let's assume a knowledge worker is responsible for planning and implementing a complex project.
>
> The knowledge worker, let's call him Max, is very confident in his abilities and believes that he can complete the project within a very tight timeframe and with limited resources. Max relies mainly on his intuition and experience to make his decisions without relying on objective data and analysis.
>
> To help Max make decisions and plan the project, an AI-based project management tool is used. This tool analyses historical data from similar projects and provides Max with objective information about the average project duration, resource utilisation and success rate. The AI also predicts potential risks and challenges Max might encounter in his project based on data from previous projects.
>
> Thanks to the AI support, Max realises that his original estimate of the project duration and the required resources was too optimistic. He adjusts his planning accordingly and takes into account the risks and challenges identified by the AI tool. Max now makes more informed decisions based on objective data and analysis, rather than relying solely on his intuition and overconfidence.
>
> Through the AI-powered project management tool, Max's overconfidence is reduced and he is able to set more realistic expectations for the project and make better decisions. This ultimately leads to a higher probability of success for the project and a more efficient use of available resources.

So by using System 4 in the above areas, knowledge workers can reduce their overconfidence by being more realistic about their skills, knowledge and decisions and by relying on objective, data-based information.

10.1.3 Availability Heuristic

Artificial intelligence (AI), particularly in the form of System 4, can help address the problem of availability heuristics among knowledge workers by analysing vast sources of information and providing the most relevant and up-to-date information. AI can search and process large amounts of data faster and more efficiently than a human, helping to reduce personal bias and enable more informed decisions.

> **Example**
> To continue the example of Max from the System 3 section, who needs to make a decision about introducing a new technology into his company: Instead of relying on the experience of his friendly colleague, Max can use AI-powered analysis to investigate various sources of information. The AI can search trade articles, research findings, testimonials from other companies and technical data sheets to get a comprehensive picture of the technology and its potential impact on the company.
> The AI can also identify potential risks and opportunities that Max might have overlooked if he had relied on the readily available information. By incorporating the information provided by the AI into his decision-making, Max is able to make a better-informed decision that is less susceptible to the availability heuristic.

By using AI systems like System 4, knowledge workers like Max can improve their decision-making and minimise the negative effects of biases like the availability heuristic. This leads to better, more objective decisions based on a broader information base.

10.1.4 Influence of Emotions on Thinking

Let's now look at the influence of emotions on thinking and decision-making and how System 4 can help reduce this problem as well. Artificial intelligence is inherently unemotional and makes decisions based on data, algorithms and statistical analysis without being influenced by emotional bias.

> **Example**
> Remember Julia from the System 3 section? Julia uses an AI-powered decision-making tool to set priorities for her team over the next few months. The tool analyses historical data, success metrics and other relevant information to make an objective recommendation for priorities. In this case, the decision is made solely based on data and algorithms, eliminating the influence of Julia's emotional charge.

AI systems can also help knowledge workers identify and correct their own emotional biases. By using AI tools to analyse decisions and discussions, users can identify possible emotional biases in their thinking and correct them accordingly.

In summary, System 4, based on artificial intelligence, can reduce the influence of emotions on thinking by making decisions based on data and algorithms, helping users to recognise and address their own emotional biases.

10.1.5 Confirmation Error

To reduce confirmation bias, System 4 can be used to perform objective and data-driven analyses that are less susceptible to personal bias. Unlike human thought processes, AI is not affected by emotions, biases or cognitive distortions that promote confirmation bias.

Some ways System 4 can address the confirmation error are:

- **Diverse sources of information:** AI systems can access extensive and diverse sources of information to provide a broader perspective and more objective assessment. This can help reduce the focus on information that confirms one's own beliefs.
- **Unbiased analysis:** AI can identify complex patterns and relationships in data without being influenced by personal beliefs or biases. By performing unbiased analysis, AI can help minimise the impact of confirmation bias.
- **Critical review:** AI can critically **review** human thought processes and decisions by presenting alternative perspectives and conflicting information. This can help to identify confirmation bias and focus on more balanced and objective decision-making.
- **Learning ability:** AI systems, especially those based on machine learning, can learn from experience and data to improve their performance over time. This can help identify confirmation bias and develop strategies to reduce its impact.

By harnessing the strengths of System 4, knowledge workers and managers can reduce the impact of confirmation bias on their decision-making and move towards more objective and informed decision-making.

10.1.6 Framing Effect

AI systems are inherently free from emotional biases and cognitive errors that can occur in human decision-makers. In the context of the framing effect, AI systems can help in the following ways:

- **Objective data analysis:** AI systems are able to analyse large amounts of data efficiently and objectively. They can integrate information from different sources and evaluate it independently of its presentation. This reduces the influence of framing on decision-making.
- **Consistent decision-making:** AI systems follow set algorithms and rules that deliver consistent and predictable results. Unlike human decision-makers, whose judgements can be influenced by emotions and cognitive biases, AI systems are immune to the framing effect.
- **Identification of biases:** Some AI systems, especially those based on machine learning, can identify patterns and biases in data. In this way, they can identify the framing effect and alert decision-makers so that they can make more informed and less biased decisions.
- **Decision support:** AI systems can act as decision support systems by presenting alternative scenarios and perspectives to human decision-makers. In this way, they can help minimise the influence of framing on decision-making and lead to a more balanced and objective assessment.

Overall, the use of AI in System 4 can help reduce the framing effect through objective data analysis, consistent decision-making, bias identification and decision support.

10.1.7 Anchor Heuristics

System 4, which is based on artificial intelligence, can help cope with the anchor heuristic in the following ways:

- **Objective analysis:** Artificial intelligence can process large amounts of data and perform objective analysis without being influenced by cognitive biases such as the anchor heuristic.
- **Identify alternatives:** AI systems can explore and evaluate a variety of alternatives to make optimal decisions without focusing on one anchor.
- **Comparison with historical data:** Artificial intelligence can identify patterns and correlations in historical data to put the influence of an anchor into perspective and enable better decisions.
- **Combining AI and human judgement:** By AI systems and human decision makers working together, the strengths of both approaches can be used to reduce the impact of anchor heuristics.

> **Example**
>
> A practical example could be an AI application in the real estate sector. An estate agent has set the price of a house at 500,000 euros. A potential buyer could focus on this anchor price and base their negotiations around it. However, an AI system based on historical data and current market conditions could perform an objective analysis of the real value of the property, taking into account factors such as location, size, condition and comparable selling prices in the area. The AI could provide the buyer with a more realistic assessment of the property's value, making the anchor price less influential in negotiations. This allows the buyer to make a more informed decision and potentially get a better deal.

10.2 Benefits for the Manager

10.2.1 Management of the New

Directly and indirectly, System 4 can offer significant benefits in the management of the new. By using AI technologies, managers and companies can benefit from the following advantages:

- **Data analytics and decision-making:** AI can analyse large amounts of data quickly and efficiently to identify patterns, trends and correlations. This information can help managers make more informed decisions when faced with new challenges and opportunities.
- **Automation of routine tasks:** AI can automate a variety of routine tasks associated with managing the new. This allows managers to focus on strategic tasks and drive innovation.
- **Forecasting and simulation:** AI models can be used to predict future developments and trends, enabling companies to be better prepared for change and adapt more efficiently.
- **Personalisation and adaptability:** AI can help to better adapt products, services and internal processes to individual customer needs and market requirements, making companies more innovative and competitive.
- **Collaboration and knowledge sharing:** AI-powered platforms can foster knowledge sharing and collaboration within organisations by capturing and harnessing the collective knowledge of employees. This can help drive innovation and develop new ideas.

A practical example of the use of System 4 in managing the new could be the use of an AI-powered idea generation and evaluation tool. The tool could collect, analyse and prioritise suggestions from employees and external partners to identify the most promising ideas for further development. By combining human creativity and AI analysis, companies can more effectively develop and implement innovative solutions based on ever-changing market conditions and customer needs.

10.2.2 Management of the Existing

Using machine learning and data-mining techniques to optimise a company's warehousing and inventory management can be categorised as managing what exists using AI. By analysing large amounts of historical data, such as sales figures, delivery times and seasonal fluctuations, an AI system can identify patterns and correlations that humans may miss. Based on this, the system can provide more accurate forecasts and recommendations for inventory planning, leading to improved efficiency and cost savings.

In the management of the existing, System 4 can be helpful in various areas:

- **Automation of routine tasks:** Artificial intelligence can help automate repetitive and time-consuming tasks, leading to greater efficiency and a reduction in the workload of employees, who can focus on higher-value tasks.
- **Big data analysis:** AI can identify patterns and correlations in big data that are difficult for humans to understand. This enables managers to make informed decisions based on these analyses and better manage their business.
- **Process optimisation:** Artificial intelligence can be used to analyse existing processes and uncover optimisation potential, for example through simulations and modelling.
- **Personalisation and customer loyalty:** AI can help to better understand customer needs and offer products and services tailored to them, which can lead to higher customer satisfaction and loyalty.

Overall, System 4 can support the management of the existing by contributing to improved efficiency, cost savings and better adaptation to customer needs through data-based analysis and automation.

10.2.3 Organisation of the Work

The book's opening quote, "Few changes have such a lasting impact on civilisation as a change in the principle on which the organisation of work is based", illustrates the profound impact that changes in the organisation of work can have on our society. System 4, based on artificial intelligence, has the potential to revolutionise the organisation of work in a way that benefits both managers and employees.

System 4 can support the organisation of work in different areas:

10   Benefits of System 4: Artificial Intelligence

- **Automation of routine activities:** Artificial intelligence can be used to automate repetitive, time-consuming tasks, leaving staff more time for more creative and strategic work.
- **Decision support:** AI systems can analyse large amounts of data and provide valuable insights that help managers make informed decisions.
- **Personalisation and adaptability:** AI systems can help tailor work environments and learning resources to the individual needs and skills of employees, increasing their motivation and performance.
- **Communication and collaboration:** AI-based tools can help improve communication and collaboration within the organisation by facilitating information sharing and enabling collaboration across geographical and temporal boundaries.

One example where System 4 can support the organisation of work is the efficient assignment of tasks to knowledge workers. Artificial intelligence can help to better identify the skills and strengths of employees and assign them to suitable projects or tasks. This can lead to higher job satisfaction, better collaboration within the team and increased productivity.

By using AI systems to analyse employee performance and preferences, managers can gain deeper insight into the individual strengths and interests of their team members. This information can be used to assign tasks and projects to the employees who are best suited for them and who are expected to be the most motivated and engaged.

For example, an AI-powered employee analytics system might determine that a particular knowledge worker is particularly good at developing creative solutions to complex problems. The manager could then target that employee to projects that require just that kind of skill to maximise the success of the project and the employee's satisfaction.

Overall, the use of System 4, that is artificial intelligence, when assigning tasks to knowledge workers can help to optimally utilise the potential of each individual employee and increase efficiency and satisfaction within the team.

10.2.4 Benefits in the Context of the Principles

System 4 can also support several of Peter Drucker's management principles, with some overlap with System 3:

- **Management by objectives (MBO):** AI-powered analytics and planning tools can help managers develop data-driven goals and strategies based on analysis of business data, market information and internal processes.
- **Delegation:** AI can be used to assign tasks and responsibilities more effectively by analysing employees' skills and competencies and finding the best matches for specific tasks.
- **Time management:** AI-powered productivity tools, such as automated scheduling and prioritisation of tasks, can help managers use their time more efficiently.
- **Effective decision-making:** AI can help managers make better decisions by analysing large amounts of data and identifying patterns, trends and relationships that are difficult for the human eye to see.
- **Focusing on strengths:** AI systems can analyse employees' individual strengths and weaknesses and help managers create targeted development plans to further build on employees' strengths.
- **Communication and collaboration:** AI can improve communication and collaboration within the organisation, for example by providing automated translations for international teams or by using chatbots to support information sharing and knowledge management.
- **Innovation and continuous improvement:** AI can help drive innovation processes, for example by identifying patterns in big data that point to new business opportunities or potential for improvement, or by supporting the implementation of innovation projects.

System 4 can thus support both similar and different principles compared to System 3. However, both systems can help to make management more effective and efficient.

10.3 Benefits for the Company

By relying on artificial intelligence, the company can more quickly and accurately identify trends and make predictions that enable it to proactively respond to changes in the market and in customer behaviour. At the same time, AI can help improve the efficiency of internal processes, for example by automating and optimising tasks, freeing up resources for customer-focused innovation.

One example is the use of AI-powered analytics tools to better understand customer behaviour and preferences. For example, a company could use machine learning and data mining to analyse customer reviews, purchase behaviour and interactions with customer service. This provides the company with valuable insights into customer needs and preferences and allows it to target its resources to develop solutions that meet those needs.

> **Summary**
> This chapter has explored the benefits of System 4, artificial intelligence, for knowledge workers, managers and businesses. Artificial intelligence can help mitigate cognitive biases by enabling objective and data-based decisions. Integrating System 4 into everyday work can help knowledge workers develop more efficient processes and reduce their workload.
>
> For the management of the new, System 4 can generate innovative ideas and solutions, while in the management of the existing it helps to optimise processes and resources. Artificial intelligence also supports the organisation of work and task completion according to Drucker's principles by enabling personalised recommendations and automated processes. Finally, System 4 can help companies better identify customer needs, target resources and develop customer-centric solutions by providing data-driven analysis and accurate forecasting.

References

Drucker, P. F. (1974). *New management practice. Volume 1 - Tasks Volume 2 - Methods*. Econ-Verlag.
Kahneman, D. (2012). *Fast thinking, slow thinking*. Siedler Verlag.

Online Sources

Wall Street Journal: IBM CEO: AI Will Be Man and Machine, Not Man vs. Machine. https://www.wsj.com/video/ibm-ceo-ai-will-be-man-and-machine-not-man-vs-machine/74769095-C3C1-4173-9269-AAE812B0D340.html?mod=Searchresults_pos11&page=1, as of 27/03/2023.

11

Concrete Application of System 4: Artificial Intelligence

11.1 Requirements and Prerequisites

11.1.1 Technological Requirements

The implementation and successful use of System 4 (artificial intelligence) requires a solid technological infrastructure and appropriate resources at the company level. This section describes the key technological requirements that companies need to meet in order to successfully deploy and use AI systems.

- **Processing power and memory:** AI systems, especially those based on machine learning and deep learning, require significant computing power and storage capacity. Companies need to ensure that they have sufficient server capacity, powerful processors and enough storage to run AI applications efficiently and process large amounts of data.
- **Network and internet connection:** A stable and fast network connection is essential for the use of AI systems, especially when it comes to cloud-based solutions or processing large amounts of data. Companies

should invest in a powerful and reliable internet connection and ensure that their network architecture is designed to meet the requirements of AI applications.
- **Data management:** Effective AI systems rely on high-quality and well-structured data. Companies need to invest in robust data management that supports the collection, storage, processing and analysis of data. This also includes the implementation of data protection measures and compliance with data protection regulations.
- **Integration and interoperability:** AI systems must be able to integrate seamlessly into existing business processes and IT systems. Companies should use open standards and interfaces to ensure the interoperability of their AI solutions with other systems and to facilitate collaboration between different departments and functions.
- **Security:** The security of AI systems is a crucial factor for the success of their implementation. Companies need to ensure that their AI applications are protected from cyber-attacks and that the integrity of the data is guaranteed. This includes the use of security protocols, encryption technologies and regular security audits.

The successful application of System 4 in companies requires a solid technological foundation that ensures both the performance and security of AI systems. By meeting the aforementioned technological requirements, companies can take full advantage of AI systems and optimise their business processes and decision-making.

11.1.2 Organisational Requirements

In addition to technological requirements, organisational factors are also crucial for successful deployment. This section therefore describes the most important organisational requirements that companies should consider in order to implement and use AI systems effectively.

11 Concrete Application of System 4: Artificial Intelligence

- **Strategic orientation and goal setting:** The introduction of AI systems should be in line with the strategic direction and goals of the company. Decision-makers should set clearly defined goals for the use of AI and develop a long-term strategy that considers both short-term and long-term use cases.
- **Organisational structure and responsibilities:** Implementing AI systems requires a clearly defined organisational structure with defined responsibilities. Companies should define roles and responsibilities for AI implementation and management, including project managers, data scientists, developers and stakeholders from different departments.
- **Change management and cultural change:** The introduction of AI systems can bring about profound changes in work processes and corporate culture. Companies should implement effective change management to ease the transition and promote employee acceptance of the new technologies. This includes communication measures, training and fostering a culture of openness and learning.
- **Training and further education:** The successful use of AI systems requires appropriate knowledge and skills on the part of employees. Companies should invest in training and education to develop employees' skills in using AI systems and provide them with the necessary tools and resources.
- **Process optimisation and automation:** The introduction of AI systems offers companies the opportunity to optimise and automate their business processes. Companies should review their existing processes and identify where AI applications add value and enable efficiency gains.

The organisational requirements for the successful implementation and use of System 4 are diverse and include aspects such as strategic orientation, organisational structure, change management, employee development and process optimisation. Companies that take these requirements into account and develop a holistic AI strategy based on them are better equipped to reap the benefits of AI systems and make their business fit for the future.

11.1.3 Data Protection and Ethical Considerations

This section aims to help companies and decision-makers understand and consider the legal and ethical requirements when implementing AI systems to ensure responsible and sustainable use of AI technologies.

With the rapid development and spread of AI systems, the requirements for the protection of personal data and the consideration of ethical aspects in the design and application of these technologies are also increasing. Companies and decision-makers need to be aware of these challenges in order to ensure responsible, legally compliant and socially acceptable use of AI.

This section aims to raise readers' awareness of the important issues of data protection and ethical considerations in the context of AI and to provide practical guidance, recommendations and examples for the successful implementation of privacy-compliant and ethically responsible AI projects.

Legal Requirements

This section provides an overview of applicable data protection laws and policies relevant to the use of AI systems, such as the General Data Protection Regulation (GDPR) in the EU.

Before we turn to the specific requirements related to artificial intelligence (System 4), we would like to emphasise that this section serves only as an initial overview and introduction to the topic of legal requirements.

It is essential to seek professional legal advice when implementing AI projects and to ensure that all relevant national and international laws and regulations are complied with.

- **General Data Protection Regulation (GDPR):** The GDPR is one of the most important legal foundations for the handling of personal data in the European Union. It sets out requirements and principles for the processing of personal data and also affects the use of AI systems, especially when they process data of EU citizens. Companies should be

aware of principles such as data minimisation, purpose limitation and transparency and ensure that AI systems comply with these principles.
- **National data protection laws:** In addition to the GDPR, companies should also consider the national data protection laws of the countries in which they operate or in which their customers are located. These laws may contain specific requirements and regulations that go beyond or complement the GDPR.
- **AI-specific laws and regulations:** In some countries and regions, legal requirements and regulations specifically for AI systems are increasingly being developed and introduced. These may include, for example, requirements for transparency, explainability, fairness or liability for AI-based decisions. Companies should keep abreast of such developments and adapt their AI projects accordingly.
- **Industry-specific regulations:** In certain industries and application areas, additional legal requirements and regulations may apply that affect the use of AI systems. Examples include the financial sector, healthcare or the public sector. It is important to take these industry-specific regulations into account and ensure that AI systems are also used in a legally compliant manner in these specific contexts.

This initial overview is intended to provide a basic understanding of the legal requirements related to AI systems. However, it is crucial to always consider the most current and relevant laws and regulations when planning and implementing AI projects and to consult legal expertise when necessary.

Ethical Principles

In his works, Peter F. Drucker repeatedly emphasised the central importance of ethical action for managers. He held the view that managers are responsible not only for the efficiency and effectiveness of the organisation but also for upholding ethical principles in their decisions and actions. Drucker made it clear that ethical action is crucial for the long-term success of a company and helps to build trust and credibility.

In this context, it is of great importance that companies using or developing artificial intelligence (AI) also pay attention to ethical principles when using System 4. As AI applications become more present in many areas of business life, it is essential to consider their potential impact on society, the environment and human rights.

In this section, we will look at the ethical principles that companies should consider when implementing and using AI systems such as System 4. In doing so, we will show how adherence to these principles helps to increase trust in AI technologies, promote their social acceptance and minimise potential risks and negative impacts.

In addition to legal requirements, ethical principles play an important role in the implementation and use of artificial intelligence (System 4). In this section, we would like to outline some basic ethical principles that companies should consider when developing and using AI systems. These principles should serve as a guide and help to deal with AI technologies in a responsible and ethically appropriate way.

- **Fairness:** AI systems should be developed and deployed in a way that avoids discrimination and promotes equal opportunities. This includes identifying and minimising potential biases in data and algorithms to ensure that AI applications do not produce unjustified or unfair results.
- **Transparency:** Companies should ensure that their AI systems are transparent by disclosing how these systems work, what data they are based on and what decision-making criteria are used. Transparent AI enables users and stakeholders to better understand and comprehend how AI systems work and their impact.
- **Accountability:** For AI systems, it should be clearly defined who is responsible for the decisions and actions taken or executed based on the AI. Companies should ensure that there are mechanisms in place to take responsibility for the results of AI applications and to take corrective action when needed.
- **Data protection and privacy:** The protection of personal data and the privacy of users and data subjects is a key ethical principle in the implementation of AI systems. Companies should ensure that they comply with legal data protection requirements and also apply best practices to protect privacy.

- **Security and reliability:** AI systems should be secure and reliable to avoid harm to people and the environment. Companies should take appropriate security measures to minimise risks such as hacking, misuse or malfunction of AI systems.
- **Human autonomy and control:** AI systems should be designed to respect and preserve human autonomy. This means that AI applications support and complement humans, rather than replacing them or restricting their freedom of choice. There should always be the possibility to ensure human control and review in AI-based decisions.

These ethical principles provide a framework to help companies develop and deploy AI systems responsibly and ethically. By taking these principles into account, companies help to strengthen trust in AI technologies and promote their social acceptance. At the same time, they can minimise potential risks and negative impacts of their AI applications.

It is important to emphasise that the ethical principles listed here are not an exhaustive list. Depending on the industry, application area and specific issues, further ethical aspects may be relevant. Companies should therefore continuously address the ethical implications of their AI applications and stay up to date in order to make responsible and ethically sound decisions.

Some organisations and countries have already developed ethical guidelines and frameworks for AI that can serve as additional guidance for companies. These include, for example, the "Ethics Guidelines for Trustworthy AI" of the European Commission or the "AI Ethics Guidelines" of the Institute of Electrical and Electronics Engineers (IEEE). In summary, companies developing or using AI systems should observe both legal requirements and ethical principles. This is the only way to ensure that AI is used in a way that is both legally compliant and in line with the values and principles of an ethically responsible society.

Data Protection Measures

This section shows practical approaches and techniques to ensure data protection when using AI, such as data anonymisation, pseudonymisation and privacy-friendly AI models.

- **Data protection measures** play a crucial role in the implementation and use of AI systems such as System 4. The processing of personal data by AI applications can entail both opportunities and risks for the privacy of data subjects. In this section, we will look at the data protection measures that companies should take to ensure privacy protection and compliance with applicable data protection laws.
- **Legal compliance:** Companies should ensure that their AI systems comply with applicable data protection laws and regulations, such as the European Data Protection Regulation (GDPR). This includes taking into account principles such as data minimisation, purpose limitation and storage limitation.
- **Data protection impact assessment:** Before introducing AI systems, companies should carry out a data protection impact assessment to identify the potential risks to the privacy of data subjects and take appropriate measures to mitigate the risks.
- **Transparency and information:** Companies should ensure that data subjects are informed about the processing of their personal data by AI systems. This includes informing them about the purpose of the processing, the underlying algorithms and the possible consequences of the processing.
- **Data security:** Companies should take appropriate technical and organisational measures to ensure the security of personal data processed. These include, for example, encryption, access controls and regular security checks.
- **Anonymisation and pseudonymisation:** Wherever possible, companies should use anonymisation and pseudonymisation to prevent or make it more difficult to identify data subjects.
- **Data portability and the right to be forgotten:** Businesses should offer data subjects the possibility to receive their personal data in a structured, commonly used and machine-readable format and, if they wish, to delete it.
- **Involvement of data protection officers:** Companies should involve data protection officers to monitor compliance with data protection regulations and ensure that data protection measures are in line with legal requirements.

11 Concrete Application of System 4: Artificial Intelligence 117

By implementing these data protection measures, companies can help increase trust in AI systems like System 4 while protecting the privacy of data subjects.

Ethical Evaluation

This section introduces methods for assessing the ethical impact of AI systems, such as ethics checks or impact assessments, and recommendations for companies to integrate ethical considerations into their AI strategy.

Ethical evaluation of AI systems such as System 4 is a crucial step in ensuring that these technologies are used responsibly and in line with society's fundamental values. Some important aspects of an ethical evaluation of AI systems are discussed below:

- **Fairness and equity:** Companies should ensure that their AI systems do not make discriminatory or unfair decisions. This can be achieved, for example, by implementing algorithms that detect and correct possible biases in the training data.
- **Transparency and accountability:** AI systems should be designed to be transparent and accountable so that external auditors and data subjects can understand and review the AI decision-making processes.
- **Accountability:** Companies should put mechanisms in place to ensure accountability for the decisions and actions of their AI systems. This can be achieved by establishing governance structures and appointing responsible individuals.
- **Protection of privacy and autonomy:** As explained in the section on data protection measures, companies should take appropriate measures to protect the privacy of data subjects and preserve their autonomy.
- **Human supervision and control:** AI systems should be designed in such a way that human supervision and control are possible and even necessary in critical situations to prevent or correct potential wrong decisions by the AI.
- **Ethics checks and impact assessments:** Companies should conduct regular ethics checks and impact assessments to evaluate the ethical

implications of their AI systems and identify potential risks. These assessments should consider both the direct and indirect impacts of AI systems on the individuals concerned and on society as a whole. Based on the results of these assessments, companies can make necessary adjustments to their systems and take measures to minimise ethical risks.

Incorporating privacy and ethical considerations into the development and implementation of AI systems such as System 4 is essential to build society's trust in these technologies and ensure that they are used for the benefit of all. Companies should be aware of the legal requirements, ethical principles and data protection measures needed to use AI responsibly and train their employees accordingly.

By being proactive in this way and conducting regular ethics checks and impact assessments, companies can not only avoid potential legal and ethical pitfalls but also strengthen their reputation as responsible players in the increasingly digitalised world. A solid foundation in data protection and ethics helps to realise the full potential of AI systems like System 4 and maximise their benefits for society at large.

11.2 Employee Competences

In the section on employee competencies, we will look at the key competencies required for the successful implementation and use of System 4, that is artificial intelligence. In doing so, we will look at various aspects that are important for employees in a company when working with artificial intelligence. The subsections of this chapter are:

- **Technical skills and expertise:** Here we cover the necessary technical knowledge and skills that employees need to work effectively with AI systems.
- **Collaboration and communication:** This section highlights the importance of collaboration and effective communication in an environment where AI systems are used to ensure that all stakeholders are well informed and work together to find solutions.

- **Critical thinking and problem-solving:** We look at the role of critical thinking and problem-solving skills when working with AI systems to ensure that employees are able to identify challenges and develop appropriate solutions.
- **Willingness to change and ability to learn:** Finally, we discuss the importance of openness to change and the ability to continuously learn and adapt when AI systems are integrated into everyday work.

11.2.1 Technical Skills and Expertise

In this section we will focus on the general skills and expertise needed to build AI systems, regardless of a specific AI product. The aim is to provide an overview of the basic skills needed to work with AI in general, rather than addressing the specific requirements of a particular product or technology.

To successfully create and apply AI systems (System 4), employees need different technical skills and expertise. We will differentiate between necessary competences for both the creation and the application of AI systems. A helpful resource for identifying and classifying the required competences is ESCO, the European Classification of Skills, Competences, Qualifications and Occupations. ESCO can help companies better understand and target the development of their employees' skills.

Creation of AI Systems

- **Fundamentals of artificial intelligence and machine learning:** Employees should have a basic understanding of the theory and principles of AI and machine learning in order to work effectively on the development of AI systems.
- **Programming skills:** Solid programming skills in languages such as Python, R or Java are crucial for the development of AI systems.
- **Data analysis and processing:** Employees must be able to analyse, prepare and process large amounts of data in order to extract valuable information for the development of AI systems.

- **Statistics and mathematics:** A good understanding of statistics and mathematics is essential to develop and optimise algorithms and models in the field of AI.
- **Modelling and optimisation:** Professionals should be able to develop, train and optimise models to achieve the best performance for the task at hand.

Application of AI Systems

- **AI system understanding:** Employees who use AI systems should have a basic understanding of how these systems work in order to use them effectively.
- **Data literacy:** A solid data literacy is necessary to effectively prepare and analyse data for AI systems.
- **Interpretation and communication of results:** Employees must be able to correctly interpret the results that AI systems provide and communicate this information to other team members and decision-makers.
- **Ethics and data protection:** An understanding of the ethical and data protection requirements in the application of AI systems is crucial in order to act responsibly and in compliance with the law.

The development and application of AI systems requires different technical skills and expertise. While some skills, such as understanding the fundamentals of AI, are relevant to both areas, there are also specific requirements for the creation and application of AI systems. By learning and developing these skills, employees can effectively contribute to the development and implementation of AI solutions in their organisation.

11.2.2 Collaboration and Communication

The successful implementation and use of AI systems (System 4) requires not only technical skills and expertise but also strong competences in the areas of collaboration and communication. Since AI systems in companies are often developed and used by interdisciplinary teams, collaboration between different departments and experts is essential.

11 Concrete Application of System 4: Artificial Intelligence

Collaboration

- **Interdisciplinary cooperation:** Employees must be able to work effectively with colleagues from different disciplines and with different expertise. This includes the ability to define common goals and organise the division of labour efficiently.
- **Teamwork:** To successfully implement AI projects, teamwork is essential. Employees must learn to recognise and use their strengths and weaknesses within a team in order to develop effective solutions together.
- **Conflict management:** When employees with different backgrounds and perspectives work together, disagreements and conflicts can arise. The ability to manage conflicts constructively and work towards a common solution is crucial for the successful implementation of AI projects.

Communication

- **Comprehensible communication:** Employees must be able to communicate technical and professional information clearly and comprehensibly both within the team and to other stakeholders. This includes the ability to explain complex issues in simple language and to use visual aids to support communication.
- **Active listening:** The ability to listen to and consider the opinions and concerns of others is essential for effective cooperation. Active listening helps to avoid misunderstandings and promotes an open and constructive working atmosphere.
- **Giving and receiving feedback:** In order to continuously learn and develop, it is important to both give and receive feedback from others. This includes constructive criticism, recognition and suggestions for improvement.
- Collaboration and communication are essential skills for employees involved in AI projects. The ability to collaborate effectively with colleagues and stakeholders and to communicate information clearly and comprehensibly contributes significantly to the success of AI systems. Companies should specifically promote these competencies when hiring and training AI staff.

11.2.3 Critical Thinking and Problem-Solving

In addition to technical expertise, collaboration and communication, critical thinking and problem-solving skills are key for employees involved in AI projects (System 4). Critical thinking enables them to question facts and contexts in order to make informed decisions and develop innovative solutions to challenges.

Critical Thinking

- **Analytical skills:** Employees must be able to analyse complex information and data to identify relationships and make informed decisions. This includes the ability to critically examine prior assumptions and hypotheses and identify possible sources of error.
- **Reflection and self-criticism:** The ability to critically reflect on one's own assumptions and actions and learn from them is essential for the continuous improvement of AI projects. Employees should be open to feedback and use it to constantly optimise their work.
- **Creative thinking:** The development of AI solutions often requires creative thinking to generate innovative approaches and ideas. Employees should be able to think outside the box and explore new ways to solve problems.

Problem-Solving

- **Identification of problems:** The ability to identify and define problems and challenges at an early stage is crucial for the success of AI projects. Staff should be able to identify both technical and organisational difficulties and develop appropriate approaches to solving them.
- **Solution-oriented thinking:** Employees should be able to approach the solution of problems in a systematic and goal-oriented way. This includes developing and evaluating different approaches to a solution, selecting the most appropriate solution and implementing that solution.
- **Adaptability:** As AI projects often take place in a dynamic environment, the ability to adapt to changes and new challenges is of great

importance. Employees should be flexible and open to change and be able to adapt their approach accordingly.

Critical thinking and problem-solving are key skills for employees involved in AI projects. The ability to analyse complex information and data, develop innovative solutions and adapt to change contributes significantly to the success of AI systems. Companies should specifically promote these competencies when hiring and training employees in the AI field.

11.2.4 Willingness to Change and Ability to Learn

In a constantly evolving world where artificial intelligence (System 4) plays an increasingly important role, the willingness of employees to change and learn is crucial for the success of companies and AI projects. Employees who are open to change and constantly willing to acquire new skills and knowledge can better adapt to the dynamic demands of AI projects and thus contribute to the success of the company.

Willingness to Change

- **Openness to new things:** Employees should be open to new technologies, processes and ways of working and see them as an opportunity to improve and develop their work.
- **Flexibility:** The ability to adapt to changes in the work environment or in project requirements is essential for the success of AI projects. Employees should be able to quickly and effectively adapt their ways of working and priorities to changing conditions.
- **Proactive attitude:** Employees should not only react to changes but also proactively look for opportunities for improvement and initiate changes if this contributes to the success of the project or the company.

Ability to Learn

- **Self-directed learning:** The ability to independently acquire new knowledge and skills is of great importance in the AI industry.

Employees should be able to identify their learning needs and take advantage of appropriate resources and training opportunities.
- **Willingness to learn:** Employees should always be willing to acquire new skills and knowledge and to continuously develop themselves. This also includes the willingness to learn from mistakes and experiences and to constantly update their own knowledge and skills.
- **Knowledge sharing and transfer:** Employees should be willing and able to share their knowledge and experience with colleagues and team members and learn from others. This promotes not only individual learning but also the collective competence of the whole team.

Willingness to change and the ability to learn are crucial competences for employees involved in AI projects. Companies should foster and support these competences by providing appropriate training opportunities and creating a culture that promotes openness to change and continuous learning.

11.3 Implementation

In the section "Implementing System 4" we will focus on the practical application of artificial intelligence (AI) in organisations. The successful implementation of System 4 requires careful planning, implementation and integration into existing work processes. In this section we will explain the different steps and aspects to be considered when implementing System 4.

First, we will look at planning and design, which involves defining the goals and requirements of the project, selecting the right AI technologies and methods and developing a project plan. In this part, we will also look at the importance of employee competencies and corporate culture to create an environment that supports and encourages AI initiatives.

In the next subchapter we will focus on the implementation of the first project. Here we will discuss the practical aspects of implementing System 4, including identifying the right project teams, working with internal and external stakeholders and continuously monitoring and adjusting the project to ensure success.

11 Concrete Application of System 4: Artificial Intelligence

Finally, we will look at the integration of System 4 into existing processes. In this part, we will discuss the challenges and opportunities in introducing artificial intelligence into everyday work, including adapting workflows, ensuring data quality and data protection and continuously improving and scaling System 4 applications.

By successfully implementing System 4, organisations can benefit from the power of artificial intelligence to develop innovative solutions to complex challenges, increase efficiency and foster a culture of collaboration and continuous learning.

11.3.1 Planning and Conception

For a project that focuses on introducing artificial intelligence (AI) into an organisation, the following specific steps should be included in the project plan:

- **Needs analysis:** Identify the specific needs and challenges of your organisation where AI applications can add value. These may include process automation, data analysis, pattern recognition or decision support.
- **Selecting AI technologies:** Investigate the available AI technologies and select those that best fit your organisation's needs and requirements. These may include machine learning, deep learning, natural language processing or image recognition.
- **Develop or customise AI solutions:** Decide whether you want to develop your own AI solution, customise an existing solution or purchase a ready-made solution from a third-party provider. Consider the resources, expertise and time required for the different options.
- **Integration into existing systems:** Ensure that the selected AI solutions can be easily integrated into your organisation's existing systems and processes. This may involve adapting the solutions to existing IT infrastructures or creating interfaces to other internal systems.
- **Training and onboarding:** Plan training and onboarding programmes for staff to provide them with the necessary knowledge and skills to

effectively use the selected AI solutions. This can include training, workshops or webinars.
- **Data protection and ethical considerations:** Consider legal data protection requirements and ethical principles when planning and implementing AI projects to ensure that user privacy is protected and AI applications are used responsibly.
- **Run a pilot project:** Launch a pilot project to test the selected AI solutions in a controlled environment and gain experience. During the pilot, continuously collect feedback from staff and other stakeholders to identify potential improvements and make adjustments. This is addressed in the section "Implement the First Project" that goes into more detail.
- **Evaluation and adjustment:** Evaluate the results of the pilot project and make adjustments to the AI solutions or processes if necessary. Take into account the experience of the users, the effectiveness of the solutions and the achievement of the project objectives. This is discussed in the section "Evaluation and Optimisation" which goes into more detail.
- **Organisation-wide introduction:** After successful completion of the pilot project and adjustments, introduce the AI solutions organisation-wide and integrate them into the daily work of the employees.
- **Monitoring and continuous improvement:** After the organisation-wide implementation of AI solutions, continuously monitor and evaluate the performance and impact of these systems. Continue to collect feedback from staff and other stakeholders to identify opportunities for improvement and adapt your AI systems accordingly.
- **Scale and adapt to change:** Over time, your organisation's requirements and needs may change. Be prepared to adapt and scale your AI solutions accordingly to continue to add value and meet changing needs.
- By following these steps, you can ensure that the implementation of AI solutions in your organisation is successful and delivers sustainable benefits. It is important to carefully plan and manage all aspects of the project to minimise risks and get the maximum benefit from the AI technologies used.

11 Concrete Application of System 4: Artificial Intelligence

11.3.2 Implement the First Project

This section is now about implementing a pilot project to test the effectiveness and feasibility of AI technology in a business context. The example project we look at in this section is the implementation of an AI-powered chatbot for customer support.

- **Define objective and scope:** The main objective of the pilot project is to improve the efficiency of customer support while reducing the workload of support staff. The chatbot should answer frequently asked questions, solve basic problems and refer customers to a human support agent if necessary. The scope of the project should be limited to a particular number of topics and questions in order to keep the implementation effort manageable.
- **Assemble project team:** Put together an interdisciplinary project team consisting of AI experts, IT staff, subject matter experts from customer support and external consultants if necessary. The team should be responsible for the development, implementation and monitoring of the chatbot.
- **Data collection and preparation:** For the training phase of the chatbot, collect data from various sources such as customer conversations, support tickets and FAQs. This data needs to be prepared and structured for the training of the chatbot model.
- **Develop and train chatbot model:** Develop the chatbot model using appropriate AI technologies and algorithms. Train the model with the processed data to optimise its ability to answer customer queries.
- **Implementation and integration:** Integrate the chatbot into the existing support infrastructure, for example on the company website or in the support app. Ensure that the chatbot works smoothly with existing systems and processes.
- **Test and evaluate:** Test the chatbot extensively to check its performance and accuracy in answering customer queries. Adjust the model as needed and improve it iteratively.
- **Rollout and monitoring:** After successful testing, the chatbot can be activated for a limited number of customers. Monitor the performance

of the chatbot continuously and collect feedback from customers and support staff to make further improvements.

A reasonable time frame for such a pilot project could be between 3 and 6 months, depending on the size and complexity of the project and the resources available to the project team.

11.3.3 Integration into Existing Processes

For the chatbot project we used as an example, integration into existing processes means the following steps:

- **Process analysis and optimisation:** Analyse the current customer care and communication processes and identify areas where the chatbot can provide an efficient solution, such as frequently asked questions, simple enquiries or making appointments. Optimise these processes by integrating the chatbot where it brings the greatest benefit.
- **Interfaces and system integration:** Ensure that the chatbot is seamlessly integrated into the existing IT infrastructure, such as CRM systems, ticketing systems and communication platforms (website, messaging services, social media etc.). This enables the chatbot to retrieve relevant information and interact efficiently with customers.
- **Change management:** Communicate openly with your staff about the introduction of the chatbot and the benefits it will bring to the business and customers. Provide training and support for employees to ease the transition and address any potential concerns.
- **Roles and responsibilities:** Clarify the responsibilities for monitoring, maintaining and improving the chatbot. Clearly define the roles of the employees who are responsible for supervising the chatbot, answering more complex customer queries and further developing the system.
- **Performance measurement and monitoring:** Develop KPIs and metrics to monitor the success of the chatbot. Measure customer satisfaction, the efficiency of query handling and the impact of the chatbot on

staff workload. Use this data to continuously improve the chatbot and adapt it to changing conditions.
- **Long-term strategy and further development:** Consider the chatbot integration as part of a long-term strategy for digitalisation and process optimisation. Plan the continuous development of the chatbot and adapt it to new technologies, business requirements and customer needs.

11.4 Evaluation and Optimisation

11.4.1 Evaluate Results

After the pilot project to implement System 4 has been completed, it is crucial to carefully evaluate the results in order to assess the success of the project and gain important insights for future AI initiatives. The evaluation of the results should be done in several steps:

- **Measure the project objectives:** Check whether the project objectives set in advance have been achieved. This can include, for example, increasing efficiency, cost savings, improving customer satisfaction or other specific key figures.
- **Analyse AI performance:** Examine the performance of the AI system by assessing its accuracy, speed and reliability. Compare these performance indicators with initial expectations and benchmarks.
- **Assess user acceptance:** Determine how well the AI system has been accepted by staff and other users. Collect feedback on usability, comprehensibility and support for decision-making or task performance.
- **Identify potential for improvement:** Identify possible weaknesses or potential for improvement of the AI system. This can concern technical aspects, user interfaces, processes or integration into existing workflows.
- **Documentation of best practices and lessons learned:** Record important findings and best practices from the pilot project in order to apply and continuously improve them in future AI initiatives.

11.4.2 Use of the Knowledge Gained

The insights that can be gained from the evaluation of the pilot project are crucial to ensure the continued success and scaling of AI initiatives in the company. The insights gained can be used in various areas:

- **Improve the AI system:** Use the insights gained to address weaknesses or potential for improvement in the technology, user interfaces or processes. This increases the efficiency, accuracy and user acceptance of the AI system.
- **Scale and expand the AI initiative:** Use the experience and best practices from the pilot to expand the implementation of AI to other departments, business units or applications. This will allow you to reap the benefits of AI technology across the entire organisation.
- **Training and further education of employees:** Use the insights gained to develop targeted training and further education measures for your employees. This promotes the acceptance and successful use of AI in your company.
- **Adjustment of corporate strategy:** The insights gained can help to review and adjust your corporate strategy and goals with regard to AI initiatives. This ensures that your AI projects are effectively aligned with your company's long-term goals.
- **Communicate the results:** Share the lessons learned and successes of the pilot internally and externally to build trust in AI technology and acceptance within the company. This can also help convince potential customers, partners or investors of the benefits of AI initiatives in your company.

11.4.3 Continuous Improvement

The aim is to constantly look for ways to further develop the AI system, processes and staff competences. The basis for this is the knowledge gained from pilot projects and ongoing AI initiatives.

To promote continuous improvement in your organisation, consider the following steps:

- **Establish a continuous learning and improvement process:** Promote a culture of learning and openness to change. Encourage your employees to actively contribute feedback, ideas and suggestions for improvement.
- **Measure and monitor the performance of your AI systems:** Use appropriate metrics and key performance indicators (KPIs) to measure the success of your AI initiatives. Monitor them continuously to identify and react to potential improvements at an early stage.
- **Conduct regular reviews and iterations:** Schedule regular reviews of AI projects and initiatives to assess progress, identify issues and make necessary adjustments. Iterative approaches such as Agile methods can help integrate continuous improvement into the project process.
- **Invest in staff training and development:** Encourage continuous training and development of your staff to improve their skills in working with AI systems and ensure the success of AI initiatives.
- **Share successes and lessons learned:** Regularly communicate the successes and lessons learned from AI projects in the company to motivate employees to learn from the experiences of others and to embed continuous improvement as part of the company culture.

Continuous improvement in the implementation of System 4 ensures that your company stays on the cutting edge of technology, uses its AI systems efficiently and effectively and strengthens its competitive position in the market in the long term.

11.5 Further Application Examples

Here are some more application examples for the use of System 4 (artificial intelligence):

- **Customer service automation:** Use AI-powered chatbots and virtual assistants to automate customer service, reduce response time and increase customer satisfaction.
- **Personalised marketing campaigns:** Use AI algorithms to create individual customer profiles and develop personalised marketing messages based on customer preferences and behaviour.

- **Process optimisation:** Identify inefficiencies and bottlenecks in your business processes with the help of AI tools and develop strategies for process optimisation and automation.
- **Fraud detection:** Use AI to detect fraud attempts and unusual activity in real time and take countermeasures.
- **Predictive maintenance:** Use AI-powered analytics to predict the condition of machinery and equipment and plan preventive maintenance to minimise unplanned downtime.
- **Personalised product recommendations:** Use AI algorithms to offer customers personalised product recommendations based on their buying behaviour and preferences.
- **Financial analysis and risk assessment:** Use AI tools to analyse financial data, assess risks and make better investment decisions.
- **Speech and text recognition:** Use AI-powered speech and text recognition systems to perform automated translations, voice control functions or sentiment analysis, for example.

These examples show that System 4 can be used in a wide range of areas and industries to automate processes, optimise decisions and increase business success. Artificial intelligence has the potential to revolutionise many aspects of the business world and offers companies the opportunity to become more competitive and efficient.

> **Checklist for the Implementation**
>
> 1. Identify goals and use cases
> Clarify which business problems or opportunities can be solved or exploited with the help of AI.
>
> 2. Consider data protection and ethical considerations
>
>   - Check legal requirements
>   - Create ethical guidelines
>   - Plan data protection measures
>
> 3. Evaluate technical and organisational requirements
>
>   - Define AI infrastructure and technology platforms
>   - Adapt organisational structures and processes

4. Promoting employee skills
   Plan training and further education measures for the use of AI systems

5. Planning and conception

   - Putting together a project team
   - Set project goals and phases
   - Plan resources and budget

6. Implement first project

   - Define success criteria and key performance indicators (KPIs)
   - Collect and process data
   - Develop and train AI models
   - Test and optimise system

7. Integration into existing processes

   - Create interfaces to other systems
   - Train and support users
   - Continuously monitor and improve AI system

8. Document and share experiences

   - Disseminate knowledge and best practices within the company
   - Analyse successes and failures to improve future AI projects

References

Online Sources

Possel, H. 1000 Citations. https://1000-zitate.de/autor/Peter+printer/, as of 27/03/2023.

Wall Street Journal: IBM CEO: AI Will Be Man and Machine, Not Man vs. Machine. https://www.wsj.com/video/ibm-ceo-ai-will-be-man-and-machine-not-man-vs-machine/74769095-C3C1-4173-9269-AAE812B0D340.html?mod=Searchresults_pos11&page=1, as of 27/03/2023.

12

Conclusion and Recommendations for Action

The best way to predict the future is to create it. —Abraham Lincoln [Poss23]

12.1 Review and Consolidation

In its various parts, the book has highlighted the range of challenges and opportunities that digitalisation and exponential change present for companies, knowledge workers and managers. The book began with an in-depth exploration of the challenges and opportunities that digitisation and exponential change present for businesses, managers and knowledge workers. Part 1 laid the foundation by addressing the pressing issues and demands of the modern workplace. Parts 2 and 3 presented System 3 and System 4 as key tools that can not only support but also enable transformative change in this complex working landscape. Both systems offer complementary strengths and opportunities to optimise decision making, problem solving and innovation.

12.2 The Relevance of System 3 and System 4

System 3, collective intelligence, has proven to be a valuable tool for collecting and processing knowledge, ideas and experiences. It promotes employee motivation and enables the development of high-quality and diverse ideas and solutions.

System 4, artificial intelligence, provides data-driven, automated solutions that help businesses respond faster and more accurately to complex challenges. Both systems complement each other in their capabilities and can be combined to increase effectiveness and efficiency in companies.

12.3 People and Technology in Management

This book has also shown that modern management strategies need to take into account not only technological but also human aspects. We have drawn on the insights of Peter F. Drucker and Daniel Kahneman to illuminate the interplay of technology and human relations in a management context.

12.4 Recommendations for Action and Next Steps

I encourage you to actively use the insights and tools presented here in your organisation. The checklists and application examples from the previous chapters can serve as a guide to help you get started using these systems and maximise the success of your projects.

12.5 Final Thoughts

The future may be uncertain, but it also offers enormous opportunities for those who are willing to accept the challenges and innovate. Digitalisation and exponential change are not only challenges but also catalysts for innovation and growth.

13

Practical Examples of AI Tools and Further Literature

In this section you will find examples of working with two very specific tools that can be used for a System 4 context.

Appendices 1 and 2 present tools that support knowledge workers on the basis of artificial intelligence. Appendix 1 shows how to work with ChatGPT and Appendix 2 on how to work with IBM Watson.

IBM Watson and ChatGPT have different deployment scenarios as they specialise in different types of tasks and applications.

IBM Watson is a comprehensive artificial intelligence and data analytics platform that is typically used for complex tasks such as analysing large amounts of data, predicting trends and patterns or developing machine learning models. IBM Watson can also be used for specific applications such as speech processing, image recognition or face recognition. IBM Watson is therefore suitable for companies and organisations that want to perform complex data analyses or develop customised applications based on machine learning and artificial intelligence.

ChatGPT, on the other hand, is a chatbot that is usually used to interact with end users. ChatGPT can be used to answer customer questions, take requests, solve problems or offer support. ChatGPT is therefore suitable for companies and organisations that need effective customer communication and want to automate interaction with their customers.

In summary, IBM Watson is mainly used for analysing and processing Big Data and developing customised applications, while ChatGPT is mainly used for automating customer communication and improving the customer experience.

In addition, there is a list of further reading in Appendix 3, each of which contains a brief description of the content of the book and takes up and elaborates on various aspects of this book.

13.1 Appendix 1: Working with ChatGPT

We will remember 2023 as the year the future began. It is the year we got access to an artificial intelligence that we can no longer talk our way out of. This time she is really intelligent. Her name is ChatGPT (Rieck, 2023).

13 Practical Examples of AI Tools and Further Literature

13.1.1 Practical Example

Have you ever wondered how companies are able to make informed decisions in today's fast-paced world? The answer lies in the combination of artificial and collective intelligence and a powerful tool called ChatGPT.

ChatGPT is an advanced AI tool that is able to understand and process natural human speech. It can respond quickly and accurately to complex questions, helping businesses work faster and more effectively. But ChatGPT is more than just a quick question-and-answer tool. It is an example of the combination of artificial and collective intelligence that is essential in today's digital world.

ChatGPT is based on large datasets and is able to recognise patterns and trends. It can automatically generate responses based on this data and is able to react to new information it learns. But that's not all ChatGPT does. It can also be monitored and trained by human experts to ensure it gives accurate and relevant responses.

But how is ChatGPT used in the context of System 4? ChatGPT complements human decision-making by providing fast and accurate answers to complex questions. It is able to process data in real time and quickly identify trends and patterns. It minimises System 1 bias by being fact and data based and minimising human bias.

Overall, ChatGPT is a powerful tool that helps companies make faster and more informed decisions. It is an example of combining artificial and collective intelligence and is an important part of System 4. If companies use ChatGPT correctly and consider the challenges it presents, they can work faster and more successfully.

So now for a practical example. I wanted to create Wordclouds for the individual sections of the book. A Wordcloud (also called a word cloud) is a visual representation of text data in which words are displayed in different sizes and colours according to their frequency or relevance.

To create a Wordcloud, the most frequent words in the text are first identified. These words are then displayed in different sizes and colours, with the size and colour of the words proportional to their frequency. The most frequent words are thus displayed larger and/or more conspicuously than less frequent words.

To do this, I had the following dialogue with ChatGPT (Vogler & ChatGPT, 2023):

aV: What tools are there for creating Wordclouds?

ChatGPT: There are many different tools you can use to create a Wordcloud. Here are some popular options:

1. Wordclouds.com: A free web app that makes it easy to create a Wordcloud from any text. You can customise the colours, fonts and sizes of the words.
2. TagCrowd: Another free tool that allows you to create a Wordcloud from any text. You can adjust the size and weight of the words to highlight their meaning.
3. Wordle: A free web app that allows you to create Wordclouds from text. Different fonts and colour schemes are available to customise the look of the Wordcloud.
4. Tableau: A data visualisation software that also supports the creation of Wordclouds. It is a powerful tool that offers many additional functions to create and analyse Wordclouds.
5. R: A programming language often used by data analysts and scientists. With the R package library you can create Wordclouds and other data visualisations.

These are just some of the tools available; there are many more options depending on your requirements and skills.

13 Practical Examples of AI Tools and Further Literature

aV: Can you create an R script for this?

ChatGPT: Yes, I can create a sample R script to create a Wordcloud from a text. Here is a simple script:

```r
# Install and load the required packages
install.packages("tm")
install.packages("wordcloud")
library(tm)
library(wordcloud)

# Path to the text file
textfile_path <- "textfile.txt"

# Read text from the file
text <- tolower(readLines(textfile_path, encoding = "UTF-8"))

# Text cleaning and preparation
text_corpus <- Corpus(VectorSource(text))
text_corpus <- tm_map(text_corpus, content_transformer(tolower))
text_corpus <- tm_map(text_corpus, removePunctuation)
text_corpus <- tm_map(text_corpus, removeNumbers)
text_corpus <- tm_map(text_corpus, removeWords, stopwords("english")) # Use
text_corpus <- tm_map(text_corpus, stripWhitespace)

# Create the word cloud
wordcloud(words = text_corpus, scale=c(3,0.5), min.freq = 5, random.order =

# Display the word cloud (in the default popup window)
```

Make sure to replace the file path in the variable `textfile_path` with the actual path to

ChatGPT: This script installs the package "wordcloud", reads in a sample text and then creates a Wordcloud from the most frequently used words in the text. You can customise the script to use your own text and customise the appearance of the Wordcloud.

aV: Can I run this under Windows?

ChatGPT: Yes, you can run the R script on Windows. Here are the steps you need to follow:

Download R for Windows and install it on your computer: https://cran.r-project.org/bin/windows/base/

Open R on your computer. You should see a console where you can enter R commands.

Copy the R script I gave you and paste it into the console.

Press the enter key to execute the script. The Wordcloud will then be generated automatically.

Please note that you may need to install the "wordcloud" package before you can run the script. This can be done with the following command in the R console:

13 Practical Examples of AI Tools and Further Literature

Once the package is installed, you can run the script and generate the Wordcloud.

aV: I get the following error when I try to install the package:
"*'install.packages' is not recognised as an internal or external command, operable program or batch file.*"
ChatGPT: This error usually occurs if the R path is not configured correctly or if R is not installed on your system. Make sure that you have installed R and R-Studio and that you have configured the path to R correctly.

If you have already installed R and R-Studio and continue to receive the error, you may need to manually add the R installation directory to your operating system path. If you are using Windows, proceed as follows:

1. Click on the "Start" button and enter "Environment variables".
2. Click on "Edit environment variables".
3. Click on "New" in the "System variables" section.
4. Enter "R_HOME" as the variable name.
5. Enter the installation directory of R as the variable value. Example: C:\Program Files\R\R-4.0.2.
6. Click on "OK" to close the "Environment Variables" window.
7. Restart R-Studio and try again to install the desired package.

aV: Thank you, that was the problem. Now it has worked.

144   A. Vogler

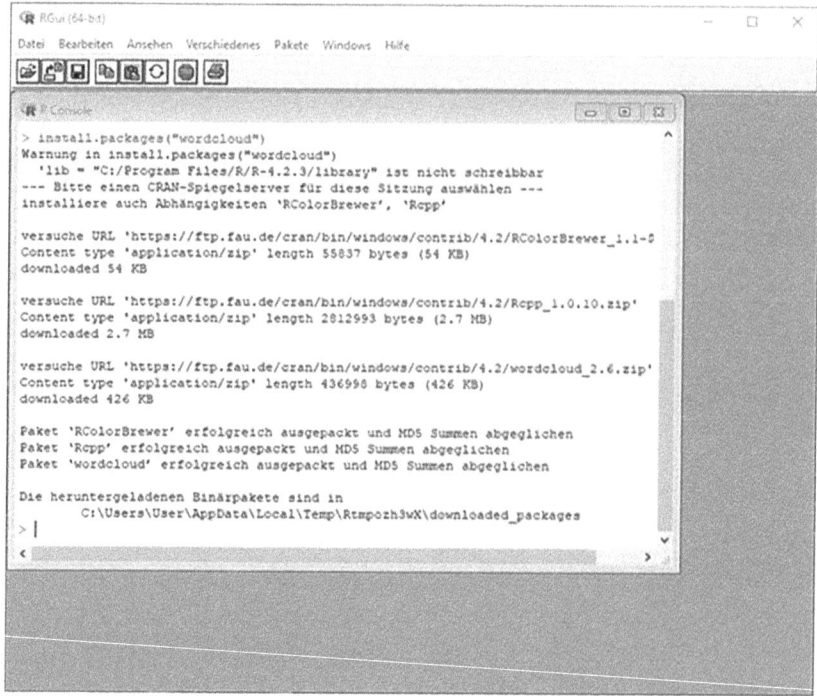

ChatGPT: Glad to hear it worked out. If you have any further questions, please don't hesitate to contact me.

aV: How do I have to change the script if the text is to be loaded from a file?

ChatGPT: To load the text from a file, you would have to adapt the script as follows:

1. Save the text in a text file, e.g. "text.txt".
2. Load the text file with the function readLines(), as in the following example:

13 Practical Examples of AI Tools and Further Literature

3. Instead of text <- "Your text here" replace this step with text <- readLines("text.txt", encoding = "UTF-8").
4. Run the script as usual.

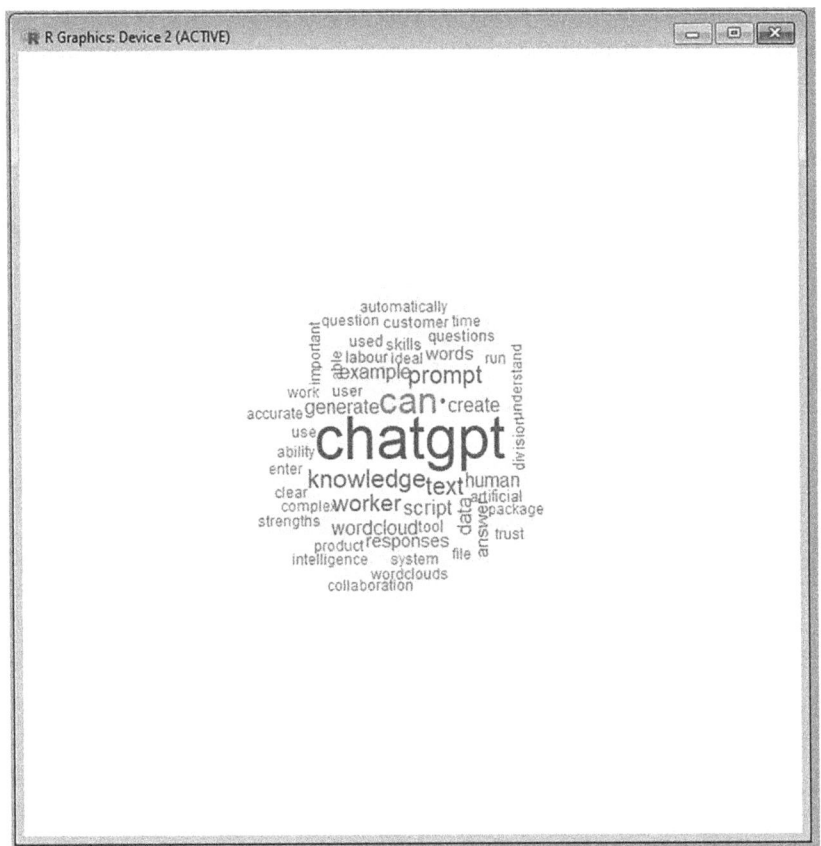

Here is a link to the Chat:
https://chat.openai.com/share/5f6cdc0c-4ddd-4a08-970f-f653874edb2c

13.1.2 Technical Terms

There are some technical terms in working with ChatGPT that the user needs to know and understand in order to work effectively with the tool. Here are some important technical terms:

- **Natural language processing (NLP):** NLP refers to ChatGPT's ability to understand and interpret human language. It enables ChatGPT to have human-like conversations and generate accurate responses.
- **Training data:** Training data are datasets used to train ChatGPT. They consist of human conversations and texts that ChatGPT uses to learn patterns and contexts and improve its ability to generate responses.
- **Dialogue management:** Dialogue management refers to ChatGPT's ability to hold a conversation and respond to the context and content of the conversation. It includes ChatGPT's ability to ask questions, give answers and respond to follow-up questions.
- **Intent recognition:** Intent recognition refers to ChatGPT's ability to understand the user's intent when asking a question or request. It enables ChatGPT to generate the most appropriate answer or recommendation.
- **API integration:** API integration refers to the integration of ChatGPT into other systems or applications via an API interface. It enables ChatGPT to generate automated responses and recommendations in other applications or systems.
- **Chatbot:** A chatbot is an application or software that has a conversation with a user. ChatGPT can be used as a chatbot to generate automated responses and recommendations.
- **Prompt:** The prompt has a very important meaning in working with ChatGPT. A prompt is a request that the user makes to ChatGPT to get an answer or recommendation. The prompt can be formulated in the form of a question, a request or a statement to which ChatGPT responds.

The prompt is a key determinant of the type of response ChatGPT generates, as it responds to the content and meaning of the prompt. A well-worded prompt can help generate accurate and useful responses, while a poorly worded prompt can lead to inaccurate or irrelevant responses.

It is important that the user formulates the prompt carefully in order to receive the best possible response or recommendation from ChatGPT. The prompt should be clearly and concisely worded to help ChatGPT understand the user's intent and generate the most appropriate response.

> **Example**
>
> Here is an example of a bad prompt and a good prompt:
>
> **Bad prompt:** "How does the product work?"
>
> This prompt is too general and non-specific to help ChatGPT generate a precise and useful response. It is unclear what product is meant and there is no specific information about what the user wants to know. A possible answer from ChatGPT could therefore be inaccurate or irrelevant.
>
> **Good prompt:** "How can I use product X more effectively to increase my productivity?"
>
> This prompt is specific and precise and gives ChatGPT clear information about what the user wants to know. It is clear which product is meant and the user has formulated a specific question that ChatGPT can answer. A possible answer from ChatGPT could provide concrete tips and recommendations on how the user can use the product more effectively to increase their productivity.
>
> Overall, it is important to formulate a clear and precise prompt to ensure that ChatGPT can generate accurate and useful responses or recommendations.

13.1.3   Division of Labour

The ideal division of labour between knowledge worker and ChatGPT depends on various factors, such as the nature of the job, the skills and experience of the knowledge worker and the strengths and weaknesses of ChatGPT. Here are some general principles that should be considered:

- **Define areas of responsibility:** It is important to define clear areas of responsibility for the knowledge worker and ChatGPT to avoid duplication and maximise efficiency. The knowledge worker should

take on tasks that require their strengths and skills, while ChatGPT should take on tasks where it excels.
- **Combination of human and artificial skills:** The ideal division of labour should optimally utilise the strengths and skills of both the knowledge worker and ChatGPT. The knowledge worker can use his human skills such as creativity, empathy and critical thinking, while ChatGPT brings in its artificial intelligence and fast information processing.
- **Flexibility and adaptability:** The ideal division of labour should be flexible and adaptable to changing needs. The knowledge worker and ChatGPT should be able to change roles or adapt their areas of responsibility, depending on needs and requirements.
- **Trust and collaboration:** A successful division of labour requires trust and collaboration between the knowledge worker and ChatGPT. The knowledge worker should trust ChatGPT and be willing to integrate it into his or her work, while ChatGPT depends on the knowledge worker's support and cooperation.

> **Example**
>
> A practical example of the ideal division of labour between a knowledge worker and ChatGPT could be in a customer service centre where ChatGPT is used to handle customer queries automatically and give knowledge workers time to deal with more complex issues.
>
> In this scenario, the knowledge worker could be responsible for the more complex customer enquiries that require more human skills, such as the ability to be empathetic, understand complex contexts and find creative solutions. The knowledge worker may also be responsible for answering questions that cannot be fully answered by ChatGPT, such as enquiries about specific product details or individual needs.
>
> ChatGPT, on the other hand, can be used to automatically process routine questions and generate standard responses. ChatGPT can answer customers' queries quickly and accurately, minimising human error and saving time. However, if ChatGPT reaches its limits or cannot fully answer a question, it can refer the case to the knowledge worker.
>
> This ideal division of labour allows knowledge workers and ChatGPT to make the most of their strengths and skills and maximise the efficiency of the customer service centre. The knowledge worker can focus on complex customer queries while ChatGPT automatically answers routine questions and frees up time for the knowledge worker. The collaboration and trust between the knowledge worker and ChatGPT can ensure seamless customer service and optimal customer care.

13 Practical Examples of AI Tools and Further Literature

Overall, the ideal division of labour between knowledge workers and ChatGPT is a combination of human and artificial capabilities based on clear lines of responsibility, flexibility, trust and collaboration. By maximising the strengths and capabilities of both parties and optimising their collaboration, they can succeed together and achieve better results.

13.2 Appendix 2: Working with IBM Watson

The cognitive era will be the beginning of a new phase in human history, where machines and humans work together to solve complex problems, where machines support human creativity and discovery, and where humans teach machines new ways of thinking and learning.—Judith Hurwitz (Hurwitz et al., 2015)

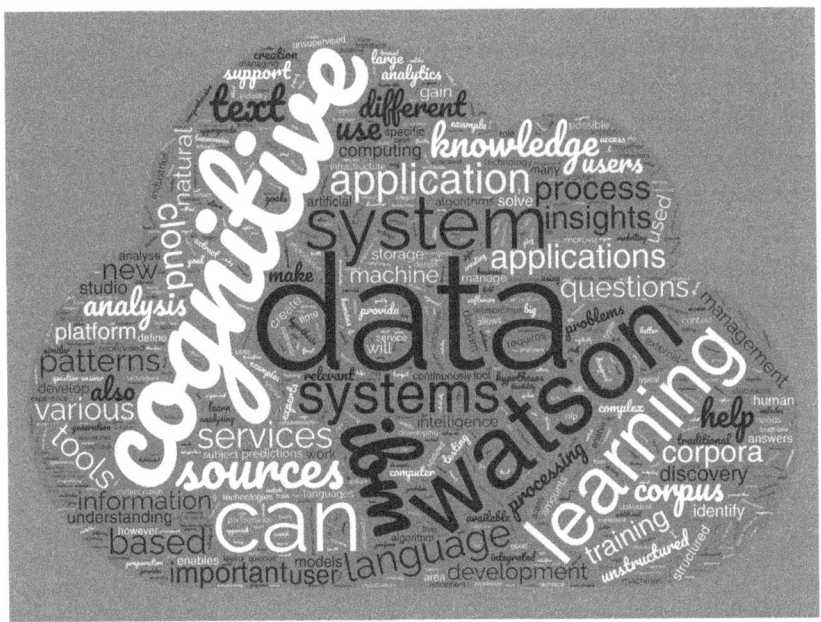

13.2.1 Cognitive Computing and Watson

This section is about working with IBM Watson. The term cognitive computing plays a major role here. IBM in particular has coined this term for all the offerings from the field of collective intelligence. The product you have certainly heard of in this context is Watson.

Cognitive computing refers to the field of artificial intelligence (AI) that aims to implement human-like cognitive capabilities in computer systems. These systems are designed to solve complex problems using natural language processing, machine learning, neural networks and other AI technologies. They process and analyse large amounts of unstructured data to identify patterns, relationships and meaning. Cognitive computing systems are able to learn from experience by processing more and more information over time and improving the quality of their predictions and decisions. They support human users by enhancing their problem-solving, decision-making and creative analysis skills. The goal of cognitive computing is to enable more natural and intuitive interaction between humans and machines and to foster collaboration that goes beyond traditional programming approaches. Thus, the topic of cognitive computing belongs in the context of System 4.

IBM Watson is an artificial intelligence platform developed by IBM based on machine learning and natural language processing. Originally known for its victory in the US quiz show *Jeopardy!* (YouTube, 2023) in 2011, Watson has since evolved into a comprehensive data analytics, cognitive services and automation solution. Watson provides powerful tools for companies in various industries such as healthcare, finance and retail to identify patterns in Big Data, improve decision-making and create personalised customer experiences. The platform is continuously evolving to support new use cases and technologies (IBM, 2020).

Watson is fundamentally different from traditional search engines. While search engines sort results by relevance based on keywords, Watson can provide targeted answers or queries to better understand the user's intent. The system thereby acts similar to a human expert.

Watson's uniqueness lies in its ability to grasp the language behind a question based on sufficient data and contextual knowledge. Through statistical analysis and predictive modelling algorithms, Watson achieves a deep understanding of the question. Instead of just a keyword search, Watson uses natural language processing (NLP) techniques to break down the question into its components and explore each component for possible answers and solutions.

This differentiated question-and-answer process, which delivers meaningful, accurate and timely answers, makes Watson unique compared to traditional search engines.

13.2.2 Cognitive Computing and Big Data Analytics

The book on which this section and the practical explanations are based is *Cognitive Computing and Big Data Analytics* by Judith Hurwitz, Marcia Kaufman and Adrian Bowles. Therefore, here is a somewhat more detailed overview of the contents of this—for me—standard work on cognitive computing (Hurwitz et al., 2015).

Cognitive systems enable humans and computers to work together to gain insight and knowledge from data by uncovering patterns and anomalies. The book is intended as a comprehensive guide that first explains the underlying technologies such as artificial intelligence, machine learning, natural language processing and Big Data analytics. It then shows how these technologies can be used to transform organisations. Various vendors and industries that are using this emerging technology to help clients gain insights and take action based on their data are presented. Detailed case studies from finance, healthcare and manufacturing illustrate the design and testing of cognitive systems.

Cognitive systems are ushering in a new era of computing. You learn how these technologies are enabling emerging companies to compete with established giants and forward-thinking incumbents to revolutionise their industries. You will receive both theoretical and practical guidance on the application of this technology, including the development of cognitive systems, the role of cloud and distributed computing, techniques for building a cognitive application and ways to use cognitive capabilities to transform your organisation. The IBM Watson platform is covered in detail as it has had a significant impact on the development of cognitive computing.

The last decade has seen tremendous technological advances. Nevertheless, the ability to extract insights and actions from data has hardly changed. In general, applications are still designed to perform predefined functions or automate business processes, so designers have to plan for each use case and programme the logic accordingly. The idea behind cognitive computing technology is to act as a partner or collaborator for human users to derive meaning from a variety of natural language texts and generate and evaluate hypotheses in seconds, based on an analysis of more data than a person could ingest in a lifetime. Traditional applications are good at automating well-defined processes. However, this approach fails when it comes to finding and using obscure relationships between data, especially in areas where the volume or complexity of data is growing rapidly. Cognitive computing technology offers a new and promising approach to application development based on software and hardware that can learn and automate cognitive tasks without reprogramming. The idea is to complement the best human skills with new application capabilities to make users not only more efficient but also more effective.

The book deals with the historical development of artificial intelligence and machine learning. Among other things, the work of Alan Turing and Norbert Weiner is presented. It explains how the human brain works and how findings from cognitive science can be transferred to computer science. The two thinking systems, "System 1" and "System 2", are introduced and the importance of a combination of both systems for cognitive computer science is emphasised. The importance of data and the importance of a flexible infrastructure for cognitive systems will also be addressed. Adaptive systems are designed to solve real-world problems in an adaptive way by analysing and relating comprehensive and complex data.

It is also about how to design and build a cognitive computer system. An important prerequisite for this is the creation of a knowledge store, called a "corpus", which comes from various data sources and can be used to support cognitive analyses. The corpus can consist of different types of data such as text documents, ontologies or taxonomies. In order to gain new insights from this data, various techniques are used, such as NLP methods or deep learning. It is also important that the system continuously learns and expands its database. The process of system development is iterative and requires cooperation between humans and machines. Overall, a cognitive computer system should provide the user with contextual insights to make informed decisions.

The different types of machine learning such as reinforcement learning and unsupervised learning are discussed. Reinforcement learning is a specific form of supervised learning where a system receives feedback on its performance to guide it towards a goal or good outcome. Unsupervised learning, on the other hand, uses statistical modelling algorithms to discover patterns or similarities in data rather than recognising them. This is most appropriate when an expert or user cannot provide examples of typical relationships or question-answer pairs to aid training. Another theme of the text is the importance of unstructured data in cognitive computing and how natural language processing (NLP) is used to extract meaning from texts and establish context. It emphasises that cognitive systems are probabilistic rather than deterministic.

The importance of statistical models such as Markov models for processing language and image understanding is explained. By using machine learning approaches such as classifiers, data can be organised into specific classes. IBM has shown with its *Jeopardy!* game that it is possible to answer questions in real time. Successful online shopping sites are characterised by a positive customer experience, which can be achieved by using NLP text analysis tools in a cognitive context. Fraud detection is an important application of NLP and cognitive computing. Big Data requires fast and efficient processing of structured and unstructured data. Hadoop is an important technology for managing Big Data. The use of analytics technologies is also important in other areas such as public health and transport. The book also describes the Digital-On-Ramps programme in Philadelphia, which aims to improve digital literacy and technical skills among residents.

Finally, the possible applications of cognitive systems in various industries such as retail, travel, transport and telecommunications are presented. It also looks at how cognitive systems can manage knowledge and what developments can be expected in the future. It is emphasised that cognitive systems will increasingly become part of the overall computer system in the future and will play an important role. The goal is to better understand and respond to user interactions and needs. However, it is emphasised that user consent will always play an important role. It is also pointed out that cognitive systems can help to recognise patterns and improve decisions in various areas.

13.2.3 Platform and Software

Platform
The IBM Watson platform is a cognitive system known for its machine learning, artificial intelligence and natural language processing capabilities. Watson is primarily available via the cloud to allow for greater scalability and flexibility, although there are also locally installable versions for specific use cases and requirements.

The IBM Watson platform is accessible via APIs (Application Programming Interfaces) that enable developers to integrate Watson services into their own applications and systems. These APIs are available through the IBM Cloud offering and developers can access them by signing up for an IBM Cloud account and selecting the appropriate Watson services as needed.

To start using the IBM Watson platform and its services, visit the IBM Cloud website: https://www.ibm.com/cloud/ . There you will find information about the available Watson services, pricing and instructions on how to get started with the platform (IBM, 2023).

Software
The IBM Cloud offers various artificial intelligence and machine learning-related services under the Watson portfolio. Some of the key Watson services include:

- **Watson Assistant:** A service for creating AI-powered chatbots and virtual assistants for customer service and internal support.
- **Watson Discovery:** A tool for automated content analysis and information extraction from large amounts of data, including unstructured text.

- **Watson Language Translator:** A service for the automatic translation of texts between different languages in real time.
- **Watson Natural Language Understanding:** A service that enables the analysis of text to identify concepts, emotions, entities, keywords, categories and semantic roles.
- **Watson Speech to Text:** An automated transcription service that converts spoken language into written text.
- **Watson Text to Speech:** A service that converts written text into spoken language and provides human-like voices in different languages and styles.
- **Watson Studio:** A platform for developing, training and managing AI and machine learning models with integrated tools and open source libraries.
- **Watson Visual Recognition:** A service that analyses images and identifies objects, faces, colours, scenes and other visual elements.

These components can be used individually or in combination to develop customised AI solutions for different use cases and industries.

13.2.4 Concept of the System

Designing a cognitive system involves developing a flexible and agile infrastructure based on machine learning, data analysis and management. It also requires specific applications that allow users to gain insights and knowledge from the system to solve complex problems in data-rich domains.

Components of a Cognitive Computing System
Infrastructure and deployment modalities: A cognitive system requires a flexible and agile infrastructure to support applications that grow over time. This includes highly parallelised and distributed environments such as cloud computing and storage services.

- **Data access, metadata and management services:** Data is at the centre of cognitive computing, so acquisition, access and management play a central role. This includes services that classify data and prepare it for use in the system.

- **Corpus, taxonomies and data catalogues:** The corpus is the knowledge base in which the recorded data is stored. It contains data in various forms and is closely linked to data access and management layers. Taxonomies and ontologies define specific entities and their relationships.
- **Data analysis services:** These services enable the understanding and analysis of the data contained in the corpus. Advanced algorithms are used to discover patterns and correlations and to make predictions.
- **Continuous machine learning:** Machine learning enables cognitive systems to learn from data without being explicitly programmed. Models are constantly updated based on new data, analyses and interactions.
- **Hypothesis generation and evaluation:** Cognitive systems develop and test hypotheses to explain observed phenomena. This is done through an iterative process of data training that may also involve human end users.
- **Learning process:** Learning from data requires tools to process both structured and unstructured data. These include natural language processing (NLP) and deep learning tools.
- **Presentation and visualisation services:** New visualisation interfaces are required to interpret complex data sets. Interactive visualisations make it possible to better understand data and recognise correlations.
- **Cognitive applications:** Cognitive systems use underlying services to create applications that solve specific problems in a particular domain. In doing so, users should be able to gain insights and knowledge from the system.

In summary, a cognitive system is designed to solve hypotheses based on learning from data. These systems are best suited for data-rich domains and help to better understand a complex world.

Building the Corpus

A corpus is a machine-readable representation of the complete dataset of a particular field or topic. Experts use corpora for tasks such as linguistic

13 Practical Examples of AI Tools and Further Literature 157

analysis to study writing styles or to determine the authenticity of a work. In cognitive systems, corpora represent the knowledge used to answer questions or discover new patterns and relationships.

The creation of a base corpus and data ingestion are crucial for the functioning of the system. A good knowledge of the application domain is necessary to determine the right data sources. The organisation of the data in the corpus influences the efficiency of the system.

During the design phase, various issues need to be addressed regarding data sources, optimisation of data organisation, integration of data from different corpora and updating of the corpus. In many fields, taxonomies and ontologies are used to represent hierarchical relationships and complex interrelationships. The choice of data structures has a great influence on system performance for recurring tasks.

The IBM Cloud offers various tools and services to create and manage corpora. Some of these tools that are useful for creating and managing corpora include:

- **IBM Watson Discovery:** Watson Discovery is a tool for analysing and processing large amounts of unstructured data. It enables the collection, storage and processing of information from various sources such as web pages, PDFs and news feeds. With Watson Discovery, users can create corpora relevant to cognitive systems by analysing text and extracting important information.
- **IBM Watson Studio:** Watson Studio is an integrated environment for developing and managing artificial intelligence, machine learning and data analytics projects. Watson Studio supports the creation and management of corpora through data preparation, modelling and collaboration tools.
- **IBM Watson Knowledge Catalog:** The Watson Knowledge Catalog is a cloud-based repository for data and AI assets that enables data to be efficiently managed, organised and shared. Users can catalogue data sources and metadata to improve data management and collaboration.
- **IBM Watson Language Translator:** The Watson Language Translator enables texts to be automatically translated into several languages, which can be helpful when creating multilingual corpora.

- **IBM Watson Speech to Text and Text to Speech:** These services enable the conversion of spoken language to text and vice versa, which can be useful when creating corpora from audio or video material.

These tools can be used individually or in combination to create and manage corpora for cognitive systems in the IBM Cloud.

Add Data to the Cognitive System

Unlike many traditional systems, the data included in the corpus is not static. You need to create a knowledge base that sufficiently defines your domain. You start filling this knowledge base with important data and continuously refine the corpus as you develop the cognitive system. Data sources are continuously added, transformed and cleansed.

Both internal and external data sources can be used to create a corpus. Organisations already manage large amounts of structured data from transactional systems and business applications, as well as unstructured data such as text and images. However, cognitive systems often need access to constantly updated, integrated data from outside the organisation. They must learn to identify and evaluate external sources and develop trust in the sources and content over time.

In various industries, such as healthcare or telecommunications, electronic datasets can provide valuable information. A cognitive system should be able to request additional data from external sources when needed to make better decisions or recommendations.

The data layer in the cognitive system is the main connection to the outside world and is responsible for importing external data. Different data formats, such as natural text, video and audio files or sensor data, have to be processed in this layer. The feature extraction layer identifies relevant data for analysis and abstracts it for machine learning.

At the data level, you work with various tools and services in the IBM Cloud to collect, store and process data. Here are some important tools you can use:

- **IBM Cloud Object Storage:** A scalable storage service for storing and managing large amounts of unstructured data such as images, videos, audio files and documents.
- **IBM Db2:** A family of database products that includes both relational and NoSQL databases suitable for storing and managing structured data.
- **IBM Cloudant:** A fully managed NoSQL database service suitable for JSON document storage and management, especially for applications requiring rapid horizontal scaling and high availability.
- **IBM Watson Studio:** A platform for collaboration between data scientists, developers and domain experts to integrate machine learning and artificial intelligence into applications.
- **IBM Watson Language Translator:** A service that uses machine learning to translate text between different languages to help analyse content from different regions and languages.
- **IBM Watson Natural Language Understanding:** A service that uses text analytics and machine learning to extract important information such as entities, concepts, emotions, sentiments and relations from unstructured text.

These tools can help you collect, store, process and integrate data from different sources into a suitable corpus for your cognitive application.

Use Machine Learning

Machine learning (ML) is a subfield of artificial intelligence that focuses on enabling computers to learn and adapt to new information and experiences without having to be explicitly programmed to do so. It is based on algorithms that can recognise patterns and correlations in the data provided and use them to make predictions or decisions.

A popular scientific approach to understanding machine learning is to compare it to human learning. For example, when a child learns to distinguish between different types of animals, it does so by seeing many examples and recognising patterns and features that are typical of each type of animal. After a certain period of time, the child can correctly assign new animals based on these learned patterns.

A similar process takes place in machine learning. An algorithm is fed a large amount of data (training data) containing examples and their associated results. The algorithm analyses this data, identifies patterns and "learns" from them. Once the algorithm is trained, it can be applied to new, previously unseen data to make predictions or classifications.

A concrete example is the automatic detection of spam emails. A machine learning algorithm is first trained with many emails that are marked as spam or non-spam. During training, the algorithm learns which features are typical for spam emails, such as certain keywords, unusual senders or conspicuous subject lines. After the algorithm has been trained, it can automatically analyse new emails and predict whether they are spam or not based on the patterns it learned during training.

Machine learning is a field that draws on methods from computer science, statistics and psychology to develop algorithms that recognise patterns in data and recommend or perform actions based on them. Two complementary approaches are supervised and unsupervised learning.

Supervised learning is based on training data that contains examples of patterns or question-answer pairs. The algorithm creates a mapping between input and output to make predictions or classifications. Application areas are classification or regression problems.

Reinforced learning is a special case of supervised learning where the system receives feedback on its performance to guide it towards a goal or good outcome. Unlike other supervised learning approaches, here the system is not explicitly trained with sample data, but learns to perform the next actions based on trial and error.

Unsupervised learning, on the other hand, uses inferential statistical modelling algorithms to discover patterns or similarities in data rather than recognising them. Unlike supervised learning, unsupervised learning is based solely on experience with the data and not on training with sample data. Unsupervised learning is appropriate when experts or users cannot provide examples of typical relationships or question-answer pairs to guide training of the system.

13 Practical Examples of AI Tools and Further Literature

Hypothesis Generation and Evaluation

In the context of cognitive computing, hypothesis generation refers to the process by which the system develops possible explanations, predictions or solutions to a given problem or issue. These hypotheses are based on available data, the system's knowledge and patterns or relationships developed through machine learning.

Cognitive computing systems are designed to mimic human-like thought processes and solve complex problems by learning and drawing conclusions from large amounts of data. Hypothesis generation is an important step in this process as it allows the system to explore different possibilities and determine the most appropriate solution based on the available information.

After a hypothesis is generated, the system can test that hypothesis by analysing further data, comparing patterns and evaluating its own performance. If the hypothesis is considered valid or useful, the system can use it to make a decision, make a recommendation or make a prediction. However, if the hypothesis is considered inaccurate or irrelevant, the system may generate further hypotheses and continue the process until it reaches a satisfactory solution.

Present the Results

A cognitive computer system generates and evaluates hypotheses and in the process can provide new answers or candidate answers for the user. The presentation of these results or questions has a great impact on the usability of the system. First, when presenting data that supports a hypothesis, the system should do so in the most understandable way possible and provide relevant evidence. Second, the user should provide additional information in a concise and unambiguous way if the system needs it.

There are three main types of services to achieve these goals:

- **Narrative solutions:** They use natural language generation techniques to tell a story about the data or summarise findings in natural language.
- **Visualisation services:** They present data in non-textual forms such as graphics, images or animations.

- **Reporting services:** They produce structured output such as database records suitable for humans or machines.

The infrastructure of a cognitive computing system includes hardware, network and storage. The two main aspects when deciding on the infrastructure are:

- **Distributed data management:** Cognitive computing systems benefit from tools that use external data resources and distribute workloads. A cloud-first strategy is recommended to ensure maximum flexibility and scalability.
- **Parallelism:** Basic hypothesis generation and evaluation can benefit from a software architecture that supports parallel generation/evaluation of multiple hypotheses. Selecting a hardware architecture that allows relatively seamless expansion with additional processors is important for system performance.

13.2.5 The Process of Implementation

The process of implementing a typical cognitive application takes place according to (Hurwitz et al., 2015) in seven steps:

1. Setting the target
2. Definition of the scope
3. Understanding of the future users
4. Questions and predictions
5. Procurement of the relevant data sources
6. Creation and refinement of the text corpora
7. Training and test

Setting the Target
The development of a cognitive application is similar in many ways to the development of other enterprise applications. First, the goals and the approach to achieve these goals must be determined. This should take into account which target groups are to be addressed and which problems

the application will solve. Unlike traditional applications, cognitive applications not only provide answers to queries but also provide deeper insights into the context and background of events.

While traditional applications often focus on business processes, the development of a cognitive application is based on knowledge and data. Therefore, the goal should be to target a specific area of an industry rather than trying to solve all the problems of an industry.

An example of a cognitive application could be in the area of financial services, with the following possible goals:

- Personalised investment recommendations based on the client's individual risk tolerance and financial goals.
- Helping clients monitor and optimise their personal finances and budgets.
- Automated analysis of market trends and their impact on investment portfolios.
- Provide up-to-date information on regulatory changes and what they mean for clients.

Cognitive applications are also ideal for helping technical support staff solve problems, for example. Take an IT company with a large and diverse group of support staff. Some employees have many years of experience and extensive knowledge to help with technical problems. However, as there is often a high turnover in such companies, many support staff lack the necessary knowledge to help customers effectively. This is where a cognitive application could be used to raise the knowledge and skills of all support staff to the level of the most experienced and competent colleagues.

Definition of the Scope

Next, the topic or subject area (the domain) for your cognitive application needs to be specified. Defining the subject area is a prerequisite for identifying and evaluating the data sources you will need for your application. In addition, defining the domain will be useful to identify the subject matter experts who can help train the system. Your goal here is to narrow down the focus of the subject area.

Cognitive systems support problem-solving in a different way than traditional systems. They are good at delivering knowledge to users quickly and efficiently. A cognitive system can provide each user with best business practices and industry-specific knowledge known to your most experienced domain experts.

The greatest value of a cognitive system is its ability to combine information from industry data sources with testing and refinement based on interactions with highly experienced experts. For example, when confronted with an unusual problem, a project manager with 30 years of experience can recall similar situations that have occurred in the past and recommend something similar to "The problem is probably A or B and we should take these five steps to get the best result".

Understanding of the Future Users
One should consider the different user groups that will use a cognitive application. Expectations of interactions influence the development of the corpus, the design of the user interface and the system training method. The accuracy required depends on the use case. For example, a scientist requires higher accuracy than someone answering questions about spare parts. However, it is not practical to anticipate all questions and applications in advance.

Cognitive applications assume a change in data quantity and quality as new sources are added. Machine learning refines question analysis and answering. Flexibility is important to adapt the application to changing user requirements. The learning process of a cognitive system is continuous, making the application smarter and more valuable as it is used.

The following best practices contribute to flexibility:

- **Understanding of user knowledge in the subject area:** Is the application for end users or experts? Do the users know technical terms? Is the application intended for user training?
- **Plan for variations in question and analysis styles:** Users of different backgrounds and knowledge may ask questions in different language styles, even if they are interested in the same topic.

- **Broad scope:** To support different types of users, the defined scope should not be too narrow or specific. A wider coverage of the subject area is more advantageous as the learning process successively optimises the corpus.

Questions and Predictions

Cognitive systems provide insights by analysing data from various sources and building models. To make a cognitive application effective, developers should consider users' potential questions, incorporating customer engagement and discovery and exploration. The application should use both question-answer pairs and anticipatory analytics to meet users' needs.

Early cognitive applications focus on advanced question-answering systems to answer questions in dialogue with the user or on analysing data to identify patterns and anomalies. The language style and expertise of end users should be taken into account to ensure effective communication and understanding.

Anticipatory cognitive systems use data to facilitate personal tasks and provide information before it is requested by the user. For example, they can monitor a user's schedule, notify when transport is delayed or support health goals.

There are several tools in the IBM Cloud that can help you define questions and explore insights:

- **IBM Watson Assistant:** Watson Assistant is an AI-powered chatbot that allows you to ask natural language questions and get answers based on available data. You can use Watson Assistant to define questions you want your cognitive system to answer and to gain insights from the data.
- **IBM Watson Discovery:** Watson Discovery helps you extract and analyse insights from Big Data. It has an intuitive user interface and AI-powered analytics that allow you to ask questions and identify patterns, trends and relationships in the data.
- **IBM Watson Studio:** Watson Studio provides you with an integrated environment in which you can develop, train and implement AI and

machine learning models. You can also use Jupyter Notebooks to analyse data, define questions and gain insights.
- **IBM Cloud Pak for Data:** This integrated data and AI platform provides various analytics and visualisation tools to help you define questions and gain insights from data. It also supports integration with Watson Discovery and Watson Assistant to explore questions and insights across multiple data sources.
- **IBM SPSS Modeler:** SPSS Modeler is an advanced data analysis and modelling tool that allows you to define questions and gain insights from your data. You can perform statistical analysis, build predictive models and identify patterns and relationships in the data.

These tools work together to help you define questions and explore insights for your cognitive applications.

Procurement of the Relevant Data Sources

When developing a corpus, it is important to identify the most relevant data sources. This is challenging as user requirements may change over time. However, it is important to evaluate both internal and external data sources and possibly develop new sources to gain new insights.

Structured data sources play an important role in cognitive computing. They provide valuable information about customers or other stakeholders in various application areas, such as travel, retail, healthcare or manufacturing. Examples of structured data sources are customer relationship management systems or electronic patient records. In addition, streaming data sources can come from sensor networks.

The analysis of so-called dark data, that is data that has been stored for years or decades but not previously analysed, can provide additional insights. With the help of machine learning, patterns can be identified in this data that enable new insights. External data sources, such as industry-specific journals, clinical trial results or industry-owned databases, can also provide important information. Many industries have standardised ontologies and taxonomies that are maintained and updated by industry consortia. These sources are crucial for the creation of a corpus and can be used specifically depending on the use case.

13 Practical Examples of AI Tools and Further Literature

There are several tools in the IBM Cloud that can help you obtain relevant data sources:

- **IBM Watson Discovery:** Watson Discovery is a powerful tool that enables you to extract, analyse and organise knowledge from a variety of data sources. It can process both structured and unstructured data and help you gather relevant information from documents, web pages, news feeds and other sources.
- **IBM Data Refinery:** Data Refinery lets you capture, cleanse, transform and connect data from multiple sources. It helps you identify and fix data quality issues so you can focus on the most relevant data.
- **IBM Cloud Pak for Data:** Cloud Pak for Data is an integrated data and AI platform that combines data integration, data management and analytics in a single environment. It enables you to collect, organise and analyse data from multiple sources to gain insights and make informed decisions.
- **IBM Watson Studio:** Watson Studio is a comprehensive platform on which you can develop, train and implement models and algorithms. It also offers data preparation functions that can help you collect and prepare your data from various sources.
- **IBM Cloud Object Storage:** This storage service allows you to store and manage large amounts of data from various sources securely and cost-effectively in the IBM Cloud. You can access this data and use it for analysis and processing by other IBM Cloud services.

These tools work together to help you obtain and manage relevant data sources for your cognitive applications.

Creation and Refinement of the Text Corpora

Developing a cognitive application requires close collaboration between the technology team and business experts. The development process starts with defining goals and user expectations, requiring extensive industry or domain knowledge. The creation of the corpus, model development, training and testing of the system require knowledge in areas such as software development, machine learning and data mining.

The corpus is not created only once, but must be continuously evaluated and updated if necessary. Data sources should be checked regularly to ensure that they are up to date. Not every data source needs to be integrated into the corpus; some can be used as cloud-based services. The process of corpus creation includes data preparation, entry, refinement and management throughout the life cycle.

During data preparation, all data must be validated and possibly transformed or annotated to make it readable, searchable and understandable. The data entry process needs to be efficient as data sources are continuously updated and expanded. The corpus should be continuously refined to ensure the accuracy of the cognitive application. Finally, data management is critical to meet privacy, security and governance requirements. Governance and security cannot be neglected in the design and operation of a cognitive system.

Several tools are available in the IBM Cloud to assist in the creation and refinement of text corpora:

- **IBM Watson Discovery:** Watson Discovery is a powerful tool that enables knowledge to be extracted, analysed and organised from a variety of data sources. It supports the processing of structured and unstructured data and can help build, refine and extend text corpora.
- **IBM Watson Natural Language Understanding (NLU):** With Watson NLU, you can analyse text corpora to extract information and insights from unstructured text data. This tool can help identify and categorise important entities, concepts, emotions and relationships in your text corpora.
- **IBM Watson Language Translator:** This tool can help you create and refine text corpora in different languages by providing machine translation between different languages.

13 Practical Examples of AI Tools and Further Literature

- **IBM Watson Studio:** Watson Studio is a comprehensive platform on which you can develop, train and implement models and algorithms. It also offers data preparation functions that can help you process and prepare your text corpora.
- **IBM Cloud Object Storage:** This storage service allows you to store and manage large volumes of text corpora securely and cost-effectively in the IBM Cloud. You can access this data and use it for analysis and processing by other IBM Cloud services.

These tools work together to help you create, refine and manage text corpora in cognitive applications.

Training and Test

Cognitive systems learn through iterative model development, analysis, training and testing. An appropriate training and testing strategy ensures that the application works properly. This involves determining the minimum acceptance accuracy and creating a ground truth that serves as the gold standard.

Erroneous answers can occur due to various factors, such as when models fail to capture nuances between similar data sources. In such cases, glossaries and ontologies can help improve.

Training and testing data is time-consuming, especially for larger and more complex domains. Sufficient data and repeated hypothesis testing are crucial to improve a cognitive system.

Various tools are available in the IBM Cloud to help with the development of cognitive systems. These include IBM Watson Studio, IBM Watson Machine Learning and IBM Watson Discovery. These tools support model development, training and testing, as well as data management and analysis.

13.3 Appendix 3: Further Reading

Allen, D.: Making It All Work. Winning at the Game of Work and the Business of Life. Viking, New York, NY, 2008.
David Allen's book *Making It All Work, Winning at the Game of Work and the Business of Life* deals with effective time management and organisational strategies based on his GTD (Getting Things Done) approach. The approach helps people get their work done more efficiently by systematically recording, prioritising and organising tasks and commitments. GTD is a system-independent, learnable process that can be adapted to different target groups.

The link to *Digital Management Practice* is that in today's digital world of exponential change and associated challenges, GTD can serve as an effective method to help managers and knowledge workers manage their tasks. The concepts and techniques presented in David Allen's book can be used in combination with the principles of collective and artificial intelligence from *Digital Management Practice* to achieve even greater efficiency in managing tasks and decision-making.

Ariely, D.: Feeling Is Useless, but It Helps. Why We Behave Irrationally Again and Again. Droemer, Munich, 2010.
In *Feeling Doesn't Help, But It Does Help*, Dan Ariely explores the different aspects of adaptation, especially hedonistic adaptation, which describes how we become accustomed to positive and negative experiences. He explains that our happiness is often short-lived and we constantly crave new things to make us happy. Ariely also emphasises the importance of risk-taking, diversity and unpredictability to achieve progress and true happiness.

In terms of *Digital Management Practice*, Ariely's research on adaptation and the pursuit of happiness can be applied to the world of work. Managers and knowledge workers can benefit from the insight that diversity, risk-taking and embracing the unpredictable contribute to innovation and personal growth. In addition, recognising that people are experiential assets can help make better staffing decisions by taking into account the complexity of employees and their potential, rather than focusing only on their CVs or specific skills.

Ariely, D.: Thinking Helps, but Is of No Use. Why We Always Make Unreasonable Decisions. Droemer, Munich, 2015.
In *Thinking May Help, but It Doesn't Help*, the author examines human irrational behaviour and decision-making processes. He emphasises that people are predictably irrational and such insights can be used to improve decision-making. Some of the topics discussed are anchors, arbitrary coherence, herd behaviour and the attraction of free offers.

In relation to *Digital Management Practice*:

- Understanding irrational behaviour can help leaders make better decisions in the context of digital transformation by considering the influence of irrational behaviour patterns.
- Anchors can be used in digital marketing to influence customers and guide their buying behaviour.

– Herd behaviour in management can help promote effective change or hinder change. Understanding this behaviour can help managers develop more targeted strategies.
– The appeal of free offers can be used in digital marketing and pricing to attract customers and increase sales.

Knowledge of these irrational behaviour patterns and their application in digital management practice can help to improve the performance of companies in an increasingly digital world and achieve competitive advantages.

Arnold, F.: Management: Learning from the Best. Hanser, Munich, 2010.

Arnold's *Management: Learning from the Best* emphasises that correct and effective decisions are achieved through the use of dissent and subsequent consensus. This involves six steps: problem identification and definition, establishing requirements, defining correctness, working out alternatives and using dissent, making decisions and building in implementation, and feedback and systematic follow-up. The importance of innovation, long-term planning and focusing on core competencies is emphasised, as is the role of feedback for continuous learning.

The link to *Digital Management Practice* is that both works emphasise the importance of knowledge, collective and artificial intelligence and the management of innovation in the digital era. Both books emphasise the need to include different perspectives and opinions in order to make better decisions and drive innovation. In addition, the importance of feedback and continuous learning is emphasised in both books to meet the ever-changing demands of the digital world.

Beckert, S.: King Cotton. A History of Global Capitalism. Beck, Munich, 2015.

In *King Cotton: A History of Global Capitalism*, Beckert examines the role of cotton in the emergence and development of capitalism. He argues that the cotton industry is a key element in understanding the modern world and the great inequalities that shape it. He introduces the term "war capitalism", which emphasises the violence and rawness of this

13 Practical Examples of AI Tools and Further Literature

process and its close connection to European imperial expansion. The cotton industry shaped both rural and urban areas and contributed to the emergence of factory owners who employed capital to target labour in the great organism of machine production. Technical progress became a constant and profits were made by increasing the productivity of human labour.

A link to *Digital Management Practice* can be made in the emphasis on the importance of innovation, technological progress and global networks. The cotton industry shows how some Europeans used capital, expertise, networks and institutions to bring about a sustained technological and material upswing. Similarly, managers and knowledge workers today need to use collective and artificial intelligence to meet the challenges of the digital age and exponential change. The history of the cotton industry also highlights the need to consider global perspectives and contexts in order to operate successfully in an increasingly interconnected world.

Chabris, C. F.; Simons, D.: The Invisible Gorilla. How Our Brain Can Be Fooled. Piper, Munich, Zurich, 2011.
The Invisible Gorilla by Chabris and Simons examines six everyday illusions that influence our thoughts and actions: attention, memory, self-confidence, knowledge, cause and possibility. These illusions can deceive us and lead us to misjudge reality.

In the context of *Digital Management Practice*, understanding these illusions is important to make better decisions and deal more effectively with the challenges of the digital world. Managers and knowledge workers should be aware of the limits of their attention, memory and cognitive abilities in order to set realistic expectations and plan for adequate resources.

By recognising these illusions, leaders can also improve their communication and collaboration, for example by communicating clearer expectations to their employees and developing a better understanding of each team member's strengths and weaknesses. Similarly, knowledge of the illusions can help optimise the use of artificial intelligence and collective intelligence to compensate for human weaknesses and cognitive biases to achieve better results.

Christensen, C. M.: The Innovator's Dilemma. Why Established Companies Lose the Competition for Breakthrough Innovations. Vahlen, Munich, 2011.
The Innovator's Dilemma by Clayton M. Christensen addresses the question of why established companies often lose the competition for breakthrough innovations. Christensen identifies the role of resources, processes and values in companies and shows that these factors can represent both success and obstacles in mastering innovation.

In the context of *Digital Management Practice*, understanding these factors is critical to successfully meeting the challenges of the digital era. Managers and knowledge workers can learn from Christensen's analysis that they need to question and adapt their processes and values to meet the fast-moving and disruptive changes.

To successfully respond to disruptive innovation, leaders should be open to change, acquire companies that have the necessary processes and values, if necessary, or create independent organisational units to address the new challenges. Artificial intelligence and collective intelligence can help support the innovation process and accelerate the identification of new market opportunities and technologies.

Overall, *The Innovator's Dilemma* shows that leaders and companies who want to succeed in the digital world must be willing to question their previous assumptions and allow changes in their processes and values in order to successfully implement breakthrough innovations.

Cole, T.: Digital Transformation. Why the German Economy Is Currently Sleeping Through the Digital Future and What Needs to Be Done Now! Vahlen, Munich, 2017.
In *Digital Transformation*, Cole describes the challenges facing the German economy to adapt to the digital future. He criticises the traditional "Nine2five" mentality, the obligation to be present and the lack of flexibility in the working world. Germany is far behind in terms of broadband expansion and many companies have no digital strategy. The digital revolution has the potential to destroy more jobs than create new ones, and Cole warns against sleeping through the digital future.

In terms of *Digital Management Practice*, Cole's work shows that German companies must learn to use modern technologies and flexible working models to remain competitive. Successful digital management involves adapting to changing conditions, using artificial intelligence and fostering a culture of trust and ownership. By adopting these principles, companies can overcome the challenges of digital transformation and succeed in the digital economy.

Cringely, R.; Cringely, R. X.: The Decline and Fall of IBM. End of an American Icon? NeRDTV, [Place of publication not identified], 2014.
In *The Decline and Fall of IBM: End of an American Icon?*, Cringely and Cringely examine the decline of IBM, once a flagship company of the American technology industry. The authors emphasise that IBM did not want to act as a mass producer of goods and therefore sold its PC division to Lenovo. IBM had difficulties establishing itself as a low-cost and at the same time high-volume manufacturer of PCs.

In terms of *Digital Management Practice*, this book shows that companies need to adapt to changing market conditions and customer expectations. IBM has failed to adapt to the challenges of the digital age, leading to its demise.

IBM Watson represents a significant development in artificial intelligence and is an example of how IBM continues to focus on innovative technologies to stay relevant in the digital age. As part of System 4, Watson enables managers and knowledge workers to gain valuable insights and make informed decisions from Big Data.

Dräger, J.; Müller-Eiselt, R.: The Digital Education Revolution. The Radical Transformation of Learning and How We Can Shape It. Dt. Verl.-Anst, Munich, 2015.
The book *The Digital Education Revolution* by Dräger and Müller-Eiselt describes the radical transformation of learning through digital technologies and how we can shape it. The authors report on their research trips and discuss innovative approaches such as personalised learning platforms, Massive Open Online Courses (MOOCs) and the use of Big Data to make education more efficient and accessible. However, they also emphasise the ethical and data protection challenges that come with digitalisation.

In terms of *Digital Management Practice*, the book shows how digital technologies and artificial intelligence are revolutionising the education system and opening up new opportunities for managers and knowledge workers to educate themselves and expand their knowledge. Personalised learning platforms and online courses enable them to continuously adapt to the challenges of the digital age and exponential change. At the same time, the importance of data protection and ethical considerations in dealing with the data collected is emphasised in order to maintain user trust and make the digital education revolution successful.

Drucker, P. F.: *New Management Practice.* Volume 1—Tasks Volume 2—Methods. Econ-Verlag, Düsseldorf, Vienna, 1974.

Drucker, P. F.: Innovations-Management für Wirtschaft und Politik. Econ-Verlag, Düsseldorf, Vienna, 1986.

Drucker, P. F.: Die postkapitalistische Gesellschaft. Econ-Verl., Düsseldorf, Vienna, New York, Moscow, 1993.

Drucker, P. F.: *The Practice of Management. A Guide to the Tasks of Management in Modern Business.* ECON, Düsseldorf, Munich, 1998.

Drucker, P. F.: Management im 21. Jahrhundert. ECON, Munich, 1999.

Drucker, P. F.: *Key Years. Stations of my Life.* Campus-Verl., Frankfurt/Main, New York, 2001.

Drucker, P. F.: *What Is Management. The Best from 50 Years.* ECON, Munich, 2002.

Dueck, G.: The New and Its Enemies. How Ideas Are Prevented and How They Still Prevail. Campus Verlag, Frankfurt am Main, 2013.
In *The New and Its Enemies*, Gunter Dueck examines how ideas are prevented and how they nevertheless prevail. Dueck emphasises that innovators meet resistance and companies are often seen as hostile. He explains that the division of labour in companies and the scientific method can hinder innovation. The book also deals with group dynamics and different roles, such as alpha, beta and omega animals, that occur in teams and their influence on innovations.

In terms of *Digital Management Practice*, this book shows that managers and knowledge workers need to be open to new ideas and overcome the resistance that often arises when they try to integrate collective and artificial intelligence into companies. They should listen to everyone's opinions without dismissing them as stupid or backward. Understanding group dynamics and the different roles of employees can help create more effective teams that foster innovation instead of blocking it.

Managers and knowledge workers should also be aware that innovation often costs more and takes longer than expected and that the transition from a prototype to a market-ready product is often challenging. Successful digital management practice therefore includes creating structures and processes that enable and support innovation, despite the obstacles that can occur in traditional working environments.

Franken, R.; Franken, S.: Integriertes Wissens- und Innovations management. With Case Studies and Examples from Corporate Practice. Gabler, Wiesbaden, 2011.
In *Integrated Knowledge and Innovation Management* by Franken and Franken, the importance of knowledge management, organisational learning and innovation management for the long-term success of a company is emphasised. The authors show how these three areas are interlinked and how together they contribute to the competitiveness and success of a company. It is emphasised that the collective intelligence of a company, which is created by many people working together, should be used to solve complex problems and develop innovative products.

In the context of *Digital Management Practice*, this literature is particularly relevant as it highlights the importance of harnessing and developing collective intelligence and knowledge within an organisation. The use of artificial intelligence and digital technologies can help companies work more efficiently, foster collaboration and drive organisational learning and innovation. By integrating knowledge and innovation management into digital management practices, managers and knowledge workers can better manage the exponential change and challenges of the digital age.

Goldin, I.: Age of Discovery. Navigating the Risks and Rewards of Our New Renaissance, 2016.
The book *Age of Discovery* by Ian Goldin examines the risks and opportunities of the new renaissance. It covers topics such as the transformation of the world of work, the role of the natural sciences and the medical application of genetics. Advances in genomics, the decoding of human

DNA and developments in proteomics have significant implications for understanding disease and treatment options.

Digital Management Practice refers to how managers and knowledge workers use technology and artificial intelligence to address challenges in the digital age. There is a connection between the topics covered in *Age of Discovery* and the challenges managers face in *Digital Management Practice*.

First, the transformation of the world of work, as described in the book, can help managers and knowledge workers develop more flexible and efficient working models by relying on temporary contracts and freelance work. These changes require a rethinking of how teams and projects are managed and organised.

Second, advances in genomics and proteomics are an example of how interdisciplinary collaboration and the use of artificial intelligence enable exponential progress. Managers and knowledge workers can use these insights to apply similar approaches in their own fields and develop innovative solutions to complex problems.

Finally, *Age of Discovery* shows how the diffusion of innovations and the interconnection of different disciplines lead to new insights and opportunities. In *Digital Management Practice*, managers and knowledge workers can use these principles to foster cross-sector collaborations, develop innovative solutions and optimise the use of artificial intelligence to better manage exponential change.

Handy, C. B.: *The Progress Trap. Giving New Meaning to the Future.* Gabler, Wiesbaden, 1995.

The book *The Progress Trap* by Charles Handy addresses the paradoxes of modern life, especially in relation to work, organisations and intelligence. Handy states that intelligence is the new form of property, but it cannot simply be distributed or bestowed by decree. He emphasises that a permanent culture of learning is necessary for the whole of society in order to overcome the growing divide between the different parts of society. In terms of *Digital Management Practice*, the book shows the importance of intelligence and creativity in the modern workplace and emphasises the need to foster a learning culture to meet the challenges of the digital age. Managers and knowledge workers should focus on the paradox of intelligence and find ways to make the best use of and promote the intellectual abilities of their employees. This also means accepting and living with the paradoxes of work and organisations to develop successful and sustainable digital management practices.

Handy, C. B.: The Elephant and the Flea. Arrow, London, 2002.
In *The Elephant and the Flea*, Charles Handy describes his personal experiences and insights as a "Flea"—an independent actor in working life. He emphasises the importance of passion for learning and the ability to define oneself and re-evaluate success. Handy notes that independence and self-reliance are increasingly important in the modern workplace and many people need to make the transition from traditional employment in large organisations (Elephants) to independent actors (Fleas).

Digital Management Practice explores how managers and knowledge workers can use collective and artificial intelligence to better meet challenges of the digital age and exponential change. Handy's book can serve as an inspiration for this practice by showing the importance of adapting to change, operating independently and flexibly and harnessing one's passion for learning. The increasing importance of independence and flexibility in the world of work highlights the need to develop and adapt new approaches to digital management in order to achieve both individual and organisational success in an ever-changing environment.

Handy, C. B.: Myself and Other More Important Matters. ECON, Berlin, 2007.
In *Myself and Other More Important Matters* Charles Handy reflects on the different roles people take on during their lives and how they deal with ethical dilemmas. Handy emphasises the importance of staying true to oneself and living a fulfilled life by finding life situations that suit one's characteristics. He also explores the difficulties that arise when professional collaboration and friendship overlap and the need to find and develop one's identity.

Digital Management Practice addresses the use of collective and artificial intelligence to meet the challenges of the digital age. In relation to Handy's book, managers and knowledge workers can benefit from his reflection on personal roles, ethics and identity. By being aware of their own strengths and weaknesses and acting authentically, they can collaborate more effectively with others and adapt to the dynamic digital work environment. In addition, distinguishing between professional and friendly relationships can help avoid potential ethical conflicts and create clearer boundaries in collaboration.

Harvard Business Manager: Leadership, What Peter Drucker already knew about the year 2020. Harvard Business Manager.

Hurwitz, J.; Kaufman, M.; Bowles, A.: Cognitive Computing and Big Data Analytics. John Wiley & Sons, New York, NY, 2015.
Cognitive Computing and Big Data Analytics by Hurwitz/Kaufmann/Bowles is a book that deals with the integration of cognitive computing technologies and Big Data analytics. The book shows how cognitive technologies such as speech processing, image recognition and machine learning can be used to optimise Big Data analytics and decision-making in companies.

The book describes how cognitive computing systems work and how they can be used in practice to automate complex tasks and gain valuable insights from large amounts of data. It also discusses the challenges and opportunities that accompany the introduction of cognitive technologies in companies.

Other topics covered in the book include the benefits of Big Data analytics and cognitive technologies for businesses, best practices for integrating cognitive technologies and Big Data analytics into business processes and the critical issues of data security and privacy. In summary, *Cognitive Computing and Big Data Analytics* provides a comprehensive overview of the integration of cognitive technologies and Big Data analytics in business. The book is aimed at both technology experts and business users who want to develop a better understanding of how cognitive computing systems can be used to make better decisions, reduce costs and increase efficiency.

Jackson, T.: Prosperity Without Growth. Living and Doing Business in a Finite World. Oekom, Munich, 2011.

In *Prosperity Without Growth*, Tim Jackson explores the paradox of happiness, where despite significant economic growth and rising GDP, life satisfaction remains unchanged in the most developed economies. Jackson questions the sustainability of perpetual growth and seeks alternative approaches to prosperity in a finite world.

Digital Management Practice refers to the use of collective and artificial intelligence to meet the challenges of the digital age and exponential change. In the context of Jackson's work, managers and knowledge workers should also think about how they can promote a sustainable and future-proof economy in a finite world. This could mean rethinking the focus on growth and instead focusing on sustainable innovations and ways of working that lead to greater prosperity and life satisfaction in the long run.

Digital Management Practice can contribute by using technology and artificial intelligence to enable more efficient, environmentally friendly and socially responsible ways of working. Managers and knowledge workers should focus on creating value beyond mere economic growth, focusing instead on aspects such as environmental protection, social justice and people's quality of life.

Kahneman, D.: *Fast Thinking, Slow Thinking*. Siedler Verlag, Munich, 2012.

Kaku, M.: *The Physics of the Future. Our Life in 100 Years*. Rowohlt, Reinbek bei Hamburg, 2012.
In *The Physics of the Future*, Michio Kaku describes what our lives could look like in 100 years. He explains that prototypes of many technologies already exist, but are unevenly distributed. Kaku examines the development of technologies such as artificial intelligence and talks about the challenges associated with their implementation. He also mentions the importance of exponential growth and Moore's Law, which states that the computing capacity of computers doubles approximately every 18 months.

Digital Management Practice and Kaku's work are closely linked, as both emphasise the importance of technology and AI in addressing the challenges of the digital age and exponential change. Managers and knowledge workers should be aware of the latest developments in technology and be prepared to use them to develop innovative solutions to problems and promote progress in the business world.

They should also focus on the ethical and social challenges associated with the implementation of AI and other advanced technologies to ensure responsible use of these technologies. As technologies such as AI become more powerful, it is important that managers and knowledge workers recognise their role in shaping a sustainable and future-proof society and address people's concerns and needs.

Kaku, M.: The Physics of Consciousness. On the Future of the Mind. Rowohlt, Reinbek bei Hamburg, 2014.
In *The Physics of Consciousness*, Michio Kaku explores the nature of the human mind and its connections to the universe. Kaku describes how the brain works and its complexity. He discusses the importance of consciousness and how it can exist in different species and even in robots. He also highlights the advances in neuroscience made possible by modern technologies such as MRI and raises the possibility that consciousness may be the fundamental basis of reality.

The link to *Digital Management Practice* is that understanding how the human brain and consciousness work, as well as advances in neuroscience and computer technology are important aspects of effectively using collective and artificial intelligence in management. New technologies, such as the brain-machine interface (BMI), enable the integration of human consciousness and machines. This integration can help to better manage the challenges of the digital age and exponential change. In addition, insights into the human brain and consciousness can help develop more effective management strategies and decision-making processes by harnessing the potential of artificial intelligence and collective thinking.

Kaufmann, T.: Business Models in Industry 4.0 and the Internet of Things. The Path from Aspiration to Reality. Springer Vieweg, Wiesbaden, 2015.
In his book *Business Models in Industry 4.0 and the Internet of Things*, Kaufmann examines the changes and innovations taking place in the course of the fourth industrial revolution. Industry 4.0 is characterised by

the use of cyber-physical systems, digital technologies and the Internet of Things, which have the potential to revolutionise business models and value chains. The combination of these technologies enables increased networking, data collection and analysis as well as automation and flexibilisation in production.

Digital Management Practice deals with the use of collective and artificial intelligence in companies to better cope with the challenges of the digital age. Both works look at how companies in Industry 4.0 are dealing with new technologies and data to develop innovative business models and achieve competitive advantages.

Kaufmann's work shows the importance of machine data and its use in Industry 4.0. It highlights how this data can be used to control processes, make decisions and ultimately enable new business models. Here lies the link to *Digital Management Practice* in that both works emphasise the importance of managers and knowledge workers making data-based decisions and harnessing the opportunities of new technologies to compete in the digital economy.

Keen, A.: *The Digital Debacle. Why the Internet Failed and How We Can Save It. Dt. Verl.-Anst; Deutsche Verlags-Anstalt, Munich, 2015.*
In *The Digital Debacle,* Keen shows the dark side of digitalisation and argues that the internet has not brought the promised benefits such as competition, transparency and diversity, but has instead led to new monopolies, data collection and surveillance. He criticises that a small elite of young, white men in Silicon Valley benefits and that the internet leads to a two-tier society in which the winners get everything and the losers go home empty-handed.

In terms of *Digital Management Practice*, it should be recognised that while the use of collective and artificial intelligence has potential to address the challenges of the digital age and exponential change, it also raises ethical and social issues. Managers and knowledge workers should therefore not only use the technical possibilities but also take responsibility for the impact of their decisions on society.

To "save" the internet, they could, for example, pay attention to transparency and data protection, reduce the digital divide and distribute wealth more equitably. In doing so, it is important to shape the tools of digitalisation in such a way that they serve society, instead of shaping them in an uncontrolled way and possibly amplifying negative effects.

Keese, C.: Silicon Valley. What's in Store for Us from the Most Powerful Valley in the World. Knaus, Munich, 2014.
In *Silicon Valley: What's in Store for Us from the Most Powerful Valley in the World*, Keese describes the disruptive innovations that Silicon Valley produces and how they challenge established business models and industries. Disruptive innovations destroy existing markets and create new ones, while sustaining innovations merely improve existing technologies. Examples of disruption are the transition from physical sound carriers to downloading and streaming in the music sector or networked cars that make traffic lights and external regulatory bodies unnecessary.

Digital Management Practice explores how managers and knowledge workers can use collective and artificial intelligence to meet the challenges of the digital age and exponential change. Keese shows in his book that established companies are often unable to recognise the need for disruption and adapt accordingly. The psyche of companies and people tends to defend what has been achieved instead of destroying and reinventing it. A link to *Digital Management Practice* is that managers must learn to understand and proactively use the mechanisms of disruption. This includes listening to customer needs, acting quickly, bringing prototypes to market and iterating continuously. It is about focusing on the essentials and avoiding unnecessary detours to meet the challenges of exponential change. Companies need to break away from traditional thought patterns and foster a culture of failure and learning through trial and error to succeed in the digital age.

Keese, C.: Silicon Germany. *How We Are Creating the Digital Transformation*. Knaus, Munich, 2016.

Laloux, F.; Laloux, F.: *Reinventing Organizations. A Guide to Designing Meaningful Forms of Cooperation*. Verlag Franz Vahlen, Munich, 2015.

13 Practical Examples of AI Tools and Further Literature

In *Reinventing Organizations*, Frederic Laloux examines the different stages of organisational development and looks at how they have changed over time. Laloux argues that each stage of human consciousness is accompanied by a breakthrough in cooperation and a new organisational model. He shows that traditional organisational models often lead to disillusionment, emptiness and stress and suggests that future models need to be adapted to the changing consciousness.

Digital Management Practice deals with the use of collective and artificial intelligence to meet the challenges of the digital age. In this context, *Reinventing Organizations* can serve as an inspiration for new organisational forms and management approaches that take into account the use of digital technologies and artificial intelligence.

Laloux's approach to developing new models can help replace traditional hierarchies and top-down structures with decentralised, democratic and participatory models. These models could use collective intelligence and the possibilities of digital technology to work together more effectively and meaningfully.

Overall, *Reinventing Organizations* encourages to question the status quo and to develop new organisational structures and models that are oriented towards the changing demands of the digital age. *Digital Management Practice* can benefit from the insights and examples in this book to develop innovative solutions to the challenges of today's business world.

Lévy, P.: *Collective Intelligence. Mankind's Emerging World in Cyberspace*. Plenum Trade, New York, 1997.

Malik, F.: Anleitung zur Selbstorganisation. Campus Verlag, Frankfurt am Main, 2012.
In *Guide to Self-Organisation*, Fredmund Malik presents his toolbox for effective general management and addresses the challenges of the knowledge age. Malik highlights the importance of a company's purpose and mission and emphasises the need to focus on customer value rather than shareholder value or stakeholder approaches. He argues that profitability and liquidity are necessary, but not the real purpose of a company. Rather,

the purpose should be the transformation of resources into benefits for the customer.

In the context of *Digital Management Practice*, Malik's work shows the importance of effective self-organisation and leadership in a digital and knowledge-based world. By emphasising customer value and effective management, companies can succeed in the digital age. The tools Malik provides can help managers and knowledge workers use collective and artificial intelligence to better manage the challenges of digital transformation and exponential change.

Malik, F.: Management. The Nuts and Bolts of the Craft. Campus-Verl., Frankfurt, M., New York, NY, 2013.
In *Management. The Nuts and Bolts of the Craft*, Fredmund Malik emphasises the importance of management as the moving force that empowers people to achieve common goals through the sharing of work and knowledge. Malik describes management as mastering complexity and refers to the growing complexity and dynamics of change in the globally interconnected world. He emphasises the application of complexity sciences such as systemics, cybernetics and bionics to effectively manage and optimise organisations. Malik emphasises that management is important for both people and organisations and calls for striving for right and good management.

In terms of *Digital Management Practice*, Malik's work shows the importance of effective management in a digital and knowledge-based world. By mastering complexity and empowering people, organisations can better meet the challenges of digital transformation. Managers and knowledge workers can benefit from the principles presented in Malik's work to harness collective and artificial intelligence and successfully meet the challenges of the digital age and exponential change.

Malik, F.: Navigating in Times of Change. Rethinking and Shaping the World. Campus-Verl., Frankfurt, M., New York, NY, 2015.
In *Navigating Times of Change*, Malik describes the challenges that managers face in a rapidly changing and complex world. The transformation of the economy and society demands new ways of thinking, tools and adaptations in organisations and management. Complexity is the raw

material for intelligence, innovation and evolution, and mastering this complexity is crucial for organisations to function. Cybernetics and self-organisation are gaining importance, while traditional management approaches are outdated.

In terms of *Digital Management Practice*, Malik's work shows the importance of adapting to digital transformation and harnessing complexity. Managers need to apply new ways of thinking and technologies such as artificial intelligence and collective intelligence to meet the challenges of the digital age. *Digital Management Practice* offers solutions to master this complexity and successfully manage change by being based on the principles of cybernetics, self-organisation and innovative approaches.

Malik, F.: Leading, Performing, Living. Effective Management for a New World. Campus Verlag, Frankfurt, 2019.
In *Leading, Performing, Living: Effective Management for a New World*, Malik presents a new approach to effective management in an ever-changing world. The book focuses on the importance of leadership, performance and living a fulfilled life in a time when traditional management concepts are no longer sufficient. To succeed in the new world, leaders must adapt to changing circumstances and draw on a combination of human skills, technological advances and systems thinking.

Digital Management Practice and Malik's book complement each other by showing that managers and knowledge workers need to use both collective and artificial intelligence to meet the challenges of the digital age and exponential change. Both emphasise the importance of adaptability, innovation and the effective use of technology to transform organisations and meet the growing demands of the digital world. Together, they offer a comprehensive perspective on management in the digital age, working towards the development of new skills, mindsets and techniques to manage complexity and change.

manager magazin: *Discoverer of Knowledge Work.* **Mastermind series: Peter F. Drucker. manager magazin, 2020.**

Mason, P.: Post-Capitalism. Grundrisse einer kommenden Ökonomie. Suhrkamp, Berlin, 2016.

In *Post-Capitalism: Outlines of a Coming Economy*, Paul Mason describes a future in which automation and networking transform large parts of work and fundamentally change ways of working. The book emphasises the need for a third management revolution that promotes the transition to networked, modular and non-linear teamwork in order to reap the benefits of collaborative and networked work.

The link to *Digital Management Practice* is that both emphasise the importance of collective and artificial intelligence and the need for change in management to meet the challenges of the digital age. While *Digital Management Practice* focuses on the application of artificial intelligence and collective thinking, Mason emphasises the need for a fundamental change in the way people work together and how organisations are managed. Both perspectives complement each other by emphasising that managers and knowledge workers must be ready to adapt to change and seize the opportunities created by digital transformation and the networked economy.

Mayer-Schönberger, V.; Cukier, K.: Big Data. The Revolution That Will Change Our Lives. Redline-Verl., Munich, 2013.
Big Data: The Revolution That Will Change Our Lives by Mayer-Schönberger and Cukier discusses the enormous amount of information being collected today and how this quantity is leading to qualitative change. Big Data makes it possible to gain new insights and create value by breaking away from traditional causal relationships and relying instead on correlations. The authors emphasise that the revolution is not in the technology, but in the data itself and the way it is analysed. Big Data is transforming numerous industries and business areas, such as healthcare and the purchase of airline tickets.

The link to *Digital Management Practice* is that both Big Data and the use of collective and artificial intelligence expand the possibilities for managers and knowledge workers to meet the challenges of the digital age and exponential change. By understanding and applying Big Data, managers and knowledge workers can make informed decisions, develop innovative solutions and respond more effectively to change. Both concepts emphasise the need to embrace the new opportunities presented by digital transformation and the explosion of data.

***Meadows, D. H.: The Limits of Thought. How We Can Recognise and Overcome Them with System.* oekom verlag, Munich, 2010.**
In *The Limits of Thought*, Meadows examines complex systems and how they affect our understanding and problem-solving. The author emphasises that system problems arise from the structures that create them and that they only disappear when we recognise and redesign these structures. Identifying the parts, linkages and functions of a system is crucial. It is equally important to align the objectives of the different sub-units of a system. In terms of *Digital Management Practice*, this book can help managers and knowledge workers better understand the systems and structures within their organisations and adapt them accordingly to meet the challenges of the digital age and exponential change. Understanding systems thinking and archetypes can help to better understand the connections between human decision-making, collective intelligence and artificial intelligence. This enables managers to consider the impact of their decisions on the whole system and thus develop more effective and sustainable solutions to the organisation's problems.

***Minto, B.: The Pyramid Principle. Logical Thinking and Formulation.* Econ-Verl., Düsseldorf, Vienna, New York, Moscow, 1993.**
Barbara Minto's book on the pyramid principle shows how to get rid of unnecessary ballast in thinking and formulating in order to write clearer business texts. It recommends separating the thinking process from the writing process and finishing the thinking before starting the writing. In order not to confuse the reader, one should keep a certain order and define the basic ideas and their sequence, while secondary ideas are properly organised to support them. It is important to identify the primary and secondary ideas and structure the relationships between them.

The book is divided into two parts: The first part teaches the pyramid principle and describes its application to build a pyramid. The second part shows how to use this knowledge to critically examine the structure of the text, discover logical breaks and encourage creative thinking so that the statement ultimately corresponds exactly to what you want to say.

A clear text takes into account the receptivity of the reader, which always has the structure of a pyramid. The human mind automatically arranges information into pyramid groupings and processes it more easily if it is already presented in this form. The number of ideas one can take in at one time is limited; therefore, one should try to move from many individual ideas to higher-level concepts. To successfully convey groupings of ideas, one must ensure that the recipient perceives them in the same way.

Minto's *The Pyramid Principle* fits well with the content of *Digital Management Practice* as it can help managers and knowledge workers to improve their communication and present complex information in a clear and understandable way. The ability to communicate effectively is crucial in a digitalised world where collaboration and collective intelligence are increasingly important.

Mumford, L.: Myth of the Machine. Culture, Technology and Power. Europaverlag, Vienna, 1974.
Myth of the Machine by Lewis Mumford looks at the role of technology in human development, in particular the impact of machines on human culture and personality. Mumford argues that technology and the machines it creates have profound effects on humanity, both positive and negative.

In terms of *Digital Management Practice*, the book can serve as a reminder that managers and knowledge workers should be aware of the potential consequences that come with the use of collective and artificial intelligence. On the one hand, technology and machines can increase efficiency and productivity, but they can also have a negative impact on human personality and culture if used in an uncontrolled manner and without regard to ethical and social concerns.

Digital Management Practice can benefit from Mumford's insights by using technology and artificial intelligence responsibly, always keeping the well-being of individuals and society in mind. This means that managers and knowledge workers should consider not only the technical possibilities and limitations but also the human and cultural aspects associated with the introduction of new technologies and ways of working.

Paz, B. J.: Kai-Fu-Lee (2019): *AI Superpowers—China, Silicon Valley and the New World Order.* AI & SOCIETY 3/35, PP. 771–772, 2020.

Rieck, C.: Schummeln mit ChatGPT: Texte verfassen mit künstlicher Intelligenz für Schule, Uni und Beruf. Also for Bing (German Edition). Yes Publishing, Munich, 2023.

Rifkin, J.: Access. The Disappearance of Property; Why We Will Own Less and Spend More. Campus-Verl., Frankfurt, 2000.
The book emphasises the shift from the importance of ownership to the importance of access and connectivity in today's world. The authors state that freedom today is less related to the ownership of material things and more related to connectedness and access to resources and opportunities. New technologies enable a globalised human experience in which intellectual capital and creativity are considered the true values of the new economy. This is shifting markets from a focus on sellers and buyers to a focus on providers and users.

In the new economy, characterised by speed and flexibility, material possessions are seen as obsolete and a hindrance. Both businesses and consumers are reorienting themselves, seeking less ownership of a thing than its availability and the ability to use it. The exchange of ownership in the marketplace is giving way to short-term access, with suppliers and customers connected in a network.

These changes in the meaning of ownership, access and networking are closely linked to the issues of *Digital Management Practice*. The book shows how managers and knowledge workers can work more effectively using collective and artificial intelligence (System 3 and System 4) to manage change and seize opportunities in a digitised world. The shift from ownership to access and connectivity highlights the importance of collaboration, collective intelligence and artificial intelligence to operate successfully in the digital age. The emphasis on intellectual capital and creativity as drivers of the new era is also a central theme in *Digital Management Practice*.

Rogers, D. L.: The Digital Transformation Playbook // Digitale Transformation im Unternehmen. Rethink Your Business for the Digital Age // Das Playbook. Columbia Business School Publishing; mitp, Frechen, 2017.

The book *The Digital Transformation Playbook* by David L. Rogers deals with digital transformation and the challenges that companies have to overcome in the digital age. Using the example of *Encyclopædia Britannica*, it illustrates that even established companies must adapt and transform in order to be successful in a digitalised world. Rogers draws an analogy to the industrial revolution and emphasises the need to overcome digital "blindspots" in order to recognise and use innovations.

In terms of *Digital Management Practice*, the book can provide important insights into how managers and knowledge workers can shape digital transformation in their companies. The need to adapt to the changes of the digital world and to rethink traditional ways of thinking and business models is a central element of *Digital Management Practice*.

To be successful in the digital age, managers and knowledge workers should critically question existing business models and processes, recognise digital technologies and innovations and implement them in their companies. This requires flexibility, openness to new things and the ability to see change as an opportunity. *Digital Management Practice* can benefit from Rogers' insights by understanding digital transformation as a continuous process and supporting and encouraging employees in this change.

Scheidler, F.: The End of the Megamachine. History of a Failing Civilisation. Promedia Verlag, Vienna, 2015.

The book *The End of the Megamachine* by Fabian Scheidler deals with the problems and challenges of our current civilisation and economy, which operates on a self-destructive path, exploiting the planet and its resources. The book shows that despite available alternatives, our society and economy are often incapable of making the necessary changes. Scheidler describes the "mega-machine" as a form of social organisation that comes up against system-immanent limits and the limits of the biosphere.

In terms of *Digital Management Practice*, the book provides important insights into the impact of our economy and technology on the environment and society. Managers and knowledge workers should use this information to make ethical and sustainable decisions in the digital age.

Digital Management Practice can benefit from Scheidler's analysis by focusing on corporate responsibility for the environment, social justice and sustainability. Managers and knowledge workers should consider the long-term impact on the environment and society in their decisions to promote a sustainable and responsible future. To do this, they can use technologies such as artificial intelligence and digital innovation to develop green solutions and accelerate the transformation towards more sustainable business models and practices.

Schmundt, H.: Gutenbergs neue Galaxis // Gutenbergs neue Galaxis - Vom Glück des digitalen Lesens. Vom Glück des digitalen Lesens // A SPIEGEL E-Book. Revised new edition. SPIEGEL-Verlag, Hamburg, 2015.

In *Gutenberg's New Galaxy*, Schmundt deals with the change in reading habits and the increasing digitalisation of books and literature. The author addresses various aspects of digital reading, such as the haptic pleasure of reading on paper, the increasing use of smartphones as reading devices and the role of technology in the book industry. Schmundt also asks whether the cultural value of a novel depends on its print substrate and discusses the opportunities and challenges posed by digital books.

Digital Management Practice and *Gutenberg's New Galaxy* are linked in that both works emphasise the need to adapt to the digital transformation and the changes it brings. In the context of *Digital Management Practice*, the insights from Schmundt's book can help to understand how reading behaviour and the use of literature are changing in the digital age. This knowledge can help managers and knowledge workers develop more effective strategies for using collective and artificial intelligence to better meet the challenges of digital transformation.

Schramm, S.; Wüstenhagen, C.: Das Alphabet des Denkens. How Language Shapes Our Thoughts and Feelings. Rowohlt, Reinbek bei Hamburg, 2015.

In *The Alphabet of Thought*, Schramm and Wüstenhagen examine the role of language in our thinking and how it shapes our thoughts and feelings. The authors look at different aspects of language research, such as the meaning of metaphors, the role of language in human experience and the study of personality through language analysis. The book is the result of a journey of discovery that begins with the smallest building blocks of words and explores the diversity of languages that exist worldwide.

Digital Management Practice and *The Alphabet of Thought* can be linked in that both works emphasise the importance of understanding and adapting to different aspects of human thought and communication. In the context of *Digital Management Practice*, understanding the role of language in our thinking and how it shapes our thoughts and feelings can help managers and knowledge workers to develop more effective communication strategies. These strategies can help improve collaboration within teams and optimise the use of collective and artificial intelligence to better meet the challenges of the digital age and exponential change.

Schwab, K.: The Fourth Industrial Revolution. Pantheon, Munich, 2016.

In *The Fourth Industrial Revolution*, Klaus Schwab describes the profound changes resulting from the interaction of technology, business and society. Schwab emphasises that leadership and an understanding of these changes are necessary to successfully manage the opportunities and challenges. He criticises the lack of institutional frameworks and argues for an overhaul of our economic, social and political systems. He also calls for a positive and unifying narrative to engage diverse individuals and communities in active co-creation and prevent resistance to the changes.

Digital Management Practice and *The Fourth Industrial Revolution* are closely linked as they both emphasise the need to address the challenges of the digital age and exponential change. *Digital Management Practice* focuses on how managers and knowledge workers can use collective and artificial intelligence to meet these challenges. Schwab's work highlights the importance of leadership and understanding the changes taking place as the Fourth Industrial Revolution unfolds. Managers and knowledge workers can gain valuable insights from this work to successfully lead

13 Practical Examples of AI Tools and Further Literature

their organisations through the digital transformation and seize the opportunities of the Fourth Industrial Revolution.

Shapiro, C.; Varian, H. R.: Online to Success. Strategy for Internet Business. Wirtschaftsverl. Langen Müller/Herbig, Munich, 1999.
In *Online to Success*, Shapiro and Varian examine economic principles that remain despite rapid technological progress. They emphasise the importance of information sources, product differentiation and understanding market structures for success in internet business. The book offers optimism and shows that despite the collapse of some old business models, many new models are waiting to be discovered and applied. The authors also discuss how giving away parts of a product or access to information can boost sales of other parts.

Digital Management Practice and *Online to Success* complement each other as they both emphasise the need to meet the challenges of the digital age and exponential change. *Digital Management Practice* focuses on the use of collective and artificial intelligence to meet these challenges. *Online to Success* offers valuable insights into economic principles and strategies that managers and knowledge workers can apply to succeed in the digital world. The combination of these insights can help managers navigate the digital transformation and successfully lead their companies into the digital age.

Silver, N.: Calculating the Future. Why Most Forecasts Are Wrong and Some Are Nevertheless True. Heyne, Munich, 2013.
Calculating the Future by Nate Silver examines why many forecasts fail and how one can nevertheless sometimes make correct predictions. The book shows that our handling of information and our ability to distinguish between valuable information and untruths is often inadequate. Moreover, we tend to focus on those signals that confirm our views and ignore the risks that are difficult to measure.

Digital Management Practice explores how collective and artificial intelligence can be used to be more successful in the digital age and exponential change. There is a clear link to Silver's work here: managers and knowledge workers can benefit from his insights by learning how to make better predictions and base their decisions on more objective information. This means that they should learn to distinguish between relevant signals and unimportant noise in order to use the flow of information more effectively and assess risks better.

Simon, F. B.: Together We Are Stupid!? The Intelligence of Companies, Managers and Markets. Carl-Auer-Systeme-Verl., Heidelberg, 2004.
In *Together We Are Stupid!?* by Fritz B. Simon, the intelligence of companies, managers and markets is examined. The author emphasises the importance of communication in social systems and argues that successful management strategies should influence the attention and observation of employees. Companies are self-organised systems that are created and maintained through selection processes. The organisational structure of a company can vary and there is no "right" form of organisation. Evolutionary systems are conservative and intelligence is limited due to the focus of attention.

Digital Management Practice explores how managers and knowledge workers can use collective and artificial intelligence to better meet the challenges of the digital age and exponential change. Simon's work is directly related to this approach as it highlights the importance of effectively managing communication and attention within organisations. Managers should be aware of how social systems work and how they can use these systems to act intelligently and responsibly. They should also recognise that different organisational structures can be successful and that there is no universal solution for all companies.

Sloan, A. P.: Meine Jahre mit General Motors. verlag moderne industrie; Verl. Moderne Industrie, Munich, 1965 // 1965 // 1966.
In *My Years with General Motors,* Sloan gives a detailed insight into the history and challenges of General Motors (GM) and its role in the development of the company. At its core, it is about the differences between centralised and decentralised organisational structures and how they affect management.

A reference to *Digital Management Practice* can be made in the way Sloan and GM dealt with the challenges of their time. Sloan emphasises that management is the key factor in ensuring the success of a company. In today's era of digitalisation and exponential change, it is equally important that managers and knowledge workers take innovative approaches to meet the challenges.

The experiences and lessons from GM's history can serve as a foundation for understanding the importance of effective management, adaptability and innovation in the digital era. The book shows how decisions and strategies made then are still relevant today when it comes to successfully managing companies in the digital age.

Digital Management Practice refers to the use of collective and artificial intelligence to manage exponential change. In doing so, managers and knowledge workers can consider the experiences and management principles described in Sloan's book and adapt them to the digital environment. This can help to better manage the challenges of digitalisation and effectively implement innovations.

Steinbicker, J.: On the Theory of the Information Society. A Comparison of the Approaches of Peter Drucker, Daniel Bell and Manuel Castells. VS Verlag für Sozialwissenschaften, Wiesbaden, 2011.
In *On the Theory of the Information Society* Steinbicker compares the approaches of Peter Drucker, Daniel Bell and Manuel Castells to the information or knowledge society. The work examines seven dimensions of a theory of the information society: new productive forces, new information and communication technologies, organisational change, structural change in work, stratification, power and social issues. Steinbicker shows that education and knowledge are becoming increasingly important, while traditional factors such as labour, capital, land, machinery and energy are becoming less important. The information society is characterised by a change in work structures, organisational models and power relations.

Digital Management Practice is concerned with the use of collective and artificial intelligence to meet the challenges of the digital age and exponential change. Steinbicker's work provides important insights into the emergence and development of the information society that are relevant for understanding *Digital Management Practice*. The seven dimensions of the information society provide a framework for examining issues such as the use of new technologies, adapting to organisational change and managing the structural transformation of work. Understanding these interrelationships enables managers and knowledge workers to develop more effective strategies for dealing with the challenges of the digital age.

Surowiecki, J.: The Wisdom of the Many. Why Groups Are Wiser Than Individuals. Goldmann, Munich, 2007.
In *The Wisdom of the Many*, Surowiecki describes how, under the right circumstances, groups can be remarkably intelligent and often smarter than the smartest individuals in their midst. He distinguishes three types of problems: cognition problems, coordination problems and cooperation problems. For group intelligence, conditions such as diversity, independence and a special kind of decentralisation are important. However, excessive communication can reduce collective intelligence, and diversity and independence of opinion are crucial, as the best collective decisions emerge from competition between independent opinions.

In terms of *Digital Management Practice*, Surowiecki's work shows the importance of accessing collective intelligence and the wisdom of the group to meet the challenges of the digital age and exponential change. Managers and knowledge workers can use the insights from *The Wisdom of the Many* to encourage group decision-making based on diversity, independence and decentralisation and to ensure that communication within the team is not excessive and reduces collective intelligence. This can lead to better and more informed decisions that meet the ever-growing demands of the digital world.

Taleb, N. N.: The Black Swan. The Power of Highly Improbable Events. Hanser, Munich, 2008.
In *The Black Swan*, Nassim Nicholas Taleb explores the power of highly improbable events and our blindness to chance, especially large deviations. Black swans are events that are rare, of enormous consequence and predictable in retrospect (but not in advance). Taleb emphasises that what we don't know is much more significant than what we do know, because black swans are often caused and exacerbated by the fact that they come unexpectedly.

In terms of *Digital Management Practice*, *The Black Swan* shows that managers and knowledge workers need to be aware of the possibility and impact of Black Swans in order to meet the challenges of the digital age and exponential change. To deal with such unpredictable events, they should focus on the adaptability, flexibility and resilience of their organisations rather than relying solely on past experience and linear predictions.

Managers and knowledge workers should learn to deal with uncertainty and adapt to scenarios that are outside their regular expectations. This includes relying on new technologies and innovative solutions to respond to unforeseen changes and challenges that may arise in the digital age.

Taleb, N. N.: Antifragile: Things that Gain from Disorder. Knaus, Munich, 2013.
In *Antifragile: Things that Gain from Disorder*, Nassim Nicholas Taleb describes the concept of antifragility, which is a unique quality of successfully dealing with the unknown without understanding it. Unlike fragility, which suffers from stress and randomness, antifragility benefits from these factors and becomes stronger. Taleb emphasises that top-down structures increase fragility, while bottom-up structures benefit from stress and disorder.

In terms of *Digital Management Practice*, antifragility implies that managers and knowledge workers should design their organisations to benefit from change, uncertainty and unpredictability in the digital age. Instead of striving only for stability and resilience, they should consider antifragility as a goal to better manage exponential change and unpredictable events.

This includes creating decentralised and flexible structures that promote adaptability and make the organisation more resilient to sudden change. Managers and knowledge workers should also establish a culture of continuous learning, experimentation and appreciation of mistakes to foster innovation and adaptability.

The use of collective and artificial intelligence can help support antifragility in organisations by enabling them to respond to unexpected events and changes without the organisation suffering. In doing so, one should acknowledge the role of chance and make a variety of small, relatively innocuous mistakes in order to be successful in the long run.

Vogler-Ludwig, K.; Düll, N.: Arbeitsmarkt 2030, // Labour Market 2030: A Strategic Foresight on Demography, Employment and Education in Germany. Bertelsmann, Bielefeld, 2013.
In *Labour Market 2030: A Strategic Foresight on Demography, Employment and Education in Germany*, Vogler-Ludwig and Düll examine demographic changes and their impact on the labour market. The authors find that the number of young and middle-aged people will decrease, while the older population will increase. Companies and labour market policy will be forced to keep older workers in the labour market longer and to adapt work organisation to changing age structures. An important aspect of this is the transfer of knowledge between older and younger employees.

In terms of *Digital Management Practice*, this means that managers and knowledge workers can use collective and artificial intelligence to meet the challenges of demographic change. Creating a work environment that promotes knowledge transfer and collaboration between different generations can help harness the experience of older employees and support the innovation of younger employees.

In addition, integrating artificial intelligence into workflows and decision-making processes can help address labour shortages by automating routine tasks and increasing the efficiency of work processes. Managers should also promote flexible working models to keep older workers in the labour market longer and use their experience for the company.

Watzlawick, P.: Münchhausens Zopf. Psychotherapy and "Reality". Huber, Bern, Stuttgart, Toronto, 1988.
In *Munchausen's Braid: Psychotherapy and "Reality"*, Paul Watzlawick examines human relationships and communication from a pragmatic perspective. He emphasises that human relationships do not exist objectively like objects, but rather are real in the view of the partners. Watzlawick also describes how every communication has two aspects: a content aspect and a relationship aspect. In relationships, conflicts can arise when partners agree on the content level but not on the relationship level.

In terms of *Digital Management Practice*, understanding human relationships and communication can be of great benefit to managers and knowledge workers to effectively navigate a digital work environment. The use of collective and artificial intelligence can help to better understand and manage communication and relationship dynamics within teams and organisations.

For example, analysing communication patterns and structures within a team through artificial intelligence can help to identify potential conflicts at an early stage and offer solutions. Managers should also be able to consider the relationship aspect of communication to create a cooperative and harmonious work environment. Integrating these insights into digital management practice can help to better manage the challenges of the digital age and exponential change.

Watzlawick, P.: Anleitung zum Unglücklichsein. Piper, Munich, Zurich, 2005.
In *Instructions for Unhappiness*, Paul Watzlawick examines the complexity of human communication and relationships. He shows how the paradoxes of communication and the so-called Be spontaneous! paradox can lead to problems and unhappiness. Watzlawick also describes how love and relationships can be affected by expectations, constraints and complications.

Digital Management Practice deals with the use of collective and artificial intelligence to better master the challenges of the digital age and exponential change. Although at first glance Watzlawick's book has no direct relation to digital management, there are important parallels:

1. Communication is a central aspect of management, and understanding the complexities and paradoxes in communication can help managers build better relationships with their staff and colleagues and avoid misunderstandings.
2. The digital world has changed communication and possibly even made it more complex. Managers should be aware of the challenges posed by digital communication and develop strategies to communicate and maintain relationships effectively.
3. The "Be spontaneous!" paradox and other paradoxes described in Watzlawick's book can also occur in digital management, for example when managers expect their teams to be innovative and spontaneous at the same time as they give them tight guidelines and directives.

In summary, Watzlawick's *Guide to Unhappiness* offers valuable insights into human communication and relationships that can also be relevant in the context of *Digital Management Practice*. By better understanding these dynamics, managers can communicate more effectively and build and lead more successful teams in the digital world.

Watzlawick, P.; Weakland, J. H.; Fisch, R.: Solutions. On the Theory and Practice of Human Change. Huber, Bern, Stuttgart, Vienna, 1984.
The book *Solutions. Zur Theorie u. Praxis menschl. Wandel* by Watzlawick, Weakland and Fisch deals with the question of how life problems arise and how some can be solved while others are complicated to the point of insolubility. The authors distinguish between two forms of change or transformation: first-order change (within a particular system) and second-order change (change in the system itself). They emphasise that many human conflicts and conflict-generating "solutions" are based on the complication between these two forms of change.

In relation to *Digital Management Practice*, the concepts of first- and second-order change are particularly relevant. Managers and knowledge workers can benefit from the insights in this book by learning to question their own assumptions and those of their organisations in order to bring about effective change. In times of the digital age and exponential change, it is important not only to look for solutions within existing systems (first-order change) but also to change the systems themselves (second-order change). This can help overcome entrenched problems and challenges by developing innovative approaches and strategies based on collective and artificial intelligence.

Weinberg, U.: Network Thinking. What Comes After Brockhaus Thinking. Murmann Verlag, Hamburg, 2015.
In *Network Thinking: What Comes After Brockhaus Thinking* by Uwe Weinberg, the concept of networked thinking is introduced, which overcomes traditional, linear patterns of thinking and adapts to increasing networking and digitalisation. The book shows how multidisciplinary thinking and the willingness to think outside the box are crucial to succeed in today's fast-paced and interconnected world.

It also emphasises the importance of creativity, quick feedback and an open culture of mistakes.

Digital Management Practice looks at how managers and knowledge workers can use collective and artificial intelligence to better manage the challenges of digitalisation and exponential change. Weinberg's *Network Thinking* complements this perspective by showing how important networked thinking and interdisciplinary collaboration are in today's working world. Both books emphasise the need to overcome rigid structures and thought patterns in order to succeed in an increasingly networked and complex world.

The insights from *Network Thinking* can be applied in *Digital Management Practice* to help organisations better adapt to the challenges of digitalisation. This can be done by fostering interdisciplinary collaboration, introducing an open error culture and using creative, networked thinking to find innovative solutions to complex problems.

References

Hurwitz, J., Kaufman, M., & Bowles, A. (2015). *Cognitive computing and big data analytics.* Wiley.

Rieck, C. (2023). *Schummeln mit ChatGPT: Texte verfassen mit künstlicher Intelligenz für Schule, Uni und Beruf.* Also for Bing (German Edition). Yes Publishing.

Online Sources

IBM. (2020). *What is Watson? IBM takes on Jeopardy.* Accessed March 28, 2023, from https://www.ibm.com/support/pages/what-watson-ibm-takes-jeopardy

IBM. (2023). *IBM cloud.* Accessed March 28, 2023, from https://www.ibm.com/cloud

Vogler, A., & ChatGPT. (2023). *Digital Management Practice Annexes.* Accessed March 28, 2023, from https://chat.openai.com/chat/2f7dd5f0-577b-46fd-9157-c3b64e4252d5

YouTube. (2023). *IBM "Watson" system to challenge humans at Jeopardy!* Accessed March 28, 2023, from https://www.youtube.com/watch?v=3e22ufcqfTs

GPSR Compliance

The European Union's (EU) General Product Safety Regulation (GPSR) is a set of rules that requires consumer products to be safe and our obligations to ensure this.

If you have any concerns about our products, you can contact us on

ProductSafety@springernature.com

In case Publisher is established outside the EU, the EU authorized representative is:

Springer Nature Customer Service Center GmbH
Europaplatz 3
69115 Heidelberg, Germany

www.ingramcontent.com/pod-product-compliance
Lightning Source LLC
LaVergne TN
LVHW041205250326
834689LV00001BA/9